STEWS

STEWS

XAVIER BRAMBLE

CONTENTS

WELCOME TO STEWS	**7**
VEG	**15**
BEANS	**41**
POULTRY	**65**
BEEF	**95**

PORK & LAMB	**129**
SEAFOOD	**171**
SIDES & SPICES	**201**
INDEX	**217**
THANKS	**222**
CONVERSION CHARTS	**223**

WELCOME TO STEWS

This is a book all about stews – stews from all corners of the world. I'm sharing my take on 80 delicious stews from around the world that I love, and I hope you will love them, too. From Nigeria to Thailand and Iran to France, we've got fresh stews, spicy stews, veggie stews, light stews, comforting stews and everything in between.

Stews are not just for winter, they aren't just comfort food and they don't (necessarily) take an age to cook. I'm here to show you why stews are brilliant and how you can make them at home, one stew at a time.

MY STORY
I grew up in north London and I always loved eating. My mother tells me that as a small child I would relentlessly throw food down me with a big grin on my face. She describes me as a gobbler.

So, it seems I've always enjoyed food, but my love for cooking didn't come about until I was at university. I arrived at my halls of residence with a few recipes up my sleeve – basic student meals: tomato pasta, egg fried rice and vegetable stir-fry among them. I also had the rough recipe for my

nan's baked chicken, which she served with rice and beans and her mouthwatering gravy. It is honestly still one of my favourite things to eat. With no one else to cook for me, I was going to learn to cook like my nan. The fire inside me was truly alight.

The day I arrived at uni, I unpacked and went straight to the local grocery store to buy the ingredients for Nan's baked chicken. I marinated it that day, then cooked it the next morning. It was awful. I remember the taste so clearly – it was massively over-seasoned. The next day I repeated the process – this time, it wasn't perfect but it was at least edible. I was already getting better at making it.

Living in my student halls with nothing much to do apart from play Fifa, drink with my flatmates or watch movies, cooking became an escape. And then it became an obsession. When I say, I became obsessed with cooking, I became OBSESSED with it. For those first six months in halls, I cooked like a madman. I was in the kitchen every day – first making really basic student meals, then taking on more complex recipes.

One day, I was in the kitchen making some oven-baked jerk chicken with rice and peas, when the incredible smoky and fiery smells that only jerk can give must have wafted down the hall, and the kitchen door burst open: 'Xav, that smells unbelievable. Can I please buy a portion?' I was confused: 'Buy?' 'Yeah,' my friend said. 'I want to buy a portion, today, tomorrow and whenever I want. It's better than going to a takeaway.' I was shocked. Six months before that, I could hardly cook and now someone wanted to pay for my food. I protested –

offered to give him a portion – but my friend insisted. In the end, we agreed on £5. He wolfed it down, told his friends, and the next day I had three people wanting the same. Then six, then eight... I couldn't believe it. People were messaging me saying they'd tried some of my food from a friend and wanted to make an order. It was surreal.

I made a small menu on Canva and posted it on a Sunday evening. The following week, I had about 15 orders. The momentum grew. It occurred to me that if I could teach myself to cook to the point that people wanted to pay for my food, I could teach others to cook, too. I downloaded TikTok and, on and off for about five months, started posting anonymised cooking videos. But I wasn't very consistent and I didn't see any results. Much later, I decided to be brave and put my face and voice out there, too. I uploaded a tuna-and-tomato pasta recipe and posted it in the evening. When I woke up, I'd had 200k views and 10k new followers. It was unbelievable. From that moment, I posted raw, unfiltered student cooking that seemed to resonate with lots of people.

To this day, the best year of my life was my university year out in Spain. I lived in Valencia, where I would study and cook during the week, then go on hikes in the surrounding hills, mountains and valleys at the weekend. I had year-round sunshine, excellent fresh fruit and wonderful produce. I also had new foods, flavours and cultures that I could explore in my cooking – not just from Spain itself, but via the people I met there, in particular new friends from South America. I was exploring world cuisine from the comfort of my own kitchen and then, in January 2023, I appeared on *Young MasterChef* on the BBC. My stay in the competition was short (I was eliminated in Round 1), but the energy I had after my appearance was amazing; I'd never felt so motivated.

In April 2023, sitting in the library in Spain, thinking about food (as usual!), my mind randomly went to stews. I didn't know much about stews back then, but I felt they were something I could make into a series. I did my research and learned pretty quickly that every country in the world has its own take on 'the stew'. I went home that day and filmed my first series episode: Puerto Rican 'Pollo Guisado'. The next day I uploaded the video and overnight it went viral, and I had hundreds of comments giving me suggestions for other stews I should make. By popular demand, 24 hours later I made a French boeuf bourguignon – that video reached 1 million views in a single day and my follower count doubled.

Returning to the UK to complete my final year at university, I had filmed over 40 stews for my series, spanning the continents and amassing a worldwide interest in the concept. I followed with Eggs from Around the World, Beans from Around the World, Ramadan from Around the World... as well as series focusing on regional dishes from the Caribbean and the Mediterranean. Companies started to notice me and, incredibly, I started to work professionally with brands.

When I graduated from university, my experience had not only given me my degree (of which I'm incredibly proud), but also a way in which I could now, stepping free from my academic life, make my passion my job. Losing no time, I booked a flight. I spent two months travelling through Asia and the Middle East with the intention of exploring new cultures and cuisines. I started off in Sri Lanka (if you're a foodie, visit Sri Lanka if you can – it's magical), then I went to the Maldives, Indonesia and Vietnam, until I ended my trip in Jordan – every stop giving me something new and inspirational for my cooking. I saw how dishes were made in family homes in Sri Lanka, in guest houses in the Maldives, and at cooking classes in Vietnam and Indonesia. I discovered desert cooking in Jordan. The trip left me with only one question: where next?

While writing this book, I had a dream come true – I arrived in Montserrat, in the West Indies, where my ancestors were born and where they lived; it was incredibly emotional. There, I made one dish that really stood out: the iconic Goat Water. It is, for sure even now, one of my favourite stews.

Throughout my adventures, I wrote my book, in the high Atlas Mountains and the Sahara Desert in Morocco, on the beaches of the Caribbean, in the forests of Indonesia, in the mountains of Vietnam, and (primarily) close to my favourite market in the world – Bolhao – in the wonderful city of Porto, Portugal. That was where I stayed for three months, wrote 80 recipes and learned so much about the unbelievable stews that Portugal has to offer.

By the time you're reading this, I have no idea where I will be. But two things are likely: I will probably be travelling and I will probably be eating a stew while I'm at it – quite simply, my two favourite things in the whole world.

ABOUT THIS BOOK

Stews for me, are the pinnacle of warmth, comfort and sharing. One bubbling pot of stew, shared between friends or loved ones, whether in the cold winters or the warm summers, is, I think, the perfect way to make memories. This book is a journey around the globe, demonstrating how – through endless preparations and permutations – every stew is a distinctive symbol of creativity. Different spices, legumes, meats and seasonal vegetables show the uniqueness of each country's cuisine, history and culture. Stews represent the skilled craftsmanship of cooks across generations – they are some of the oldest concepts of food, a staple of cuisines around the world for centuries. In this book, I wanted to share with the world the journey that led me to fall in love with stew, and to show how every stew has allowed me, not only to reflect on each country's special traditions manifested in its foods, but to develop and express my own creativity in the kitchen.

The fundamental beauty of a stew lies, I think, in its versatility. I've organised the chapters according to the main component of each dish – **VEG**, **BEANS**, **POULTRY**, **BEEF**, **PORK & LAMB** and **SEAFOOD**. Throughout, you'll find stews for every occasion – whether you're looking for a quick-and-easy midweek bite or something slower for those cosy Sunday evenings, they are all here. There are stews with easy-to-find or only a few ingredients for when you're short of time, and stews with harder-to-source ingredients or more complex flavours for when you feel like more of a challenge. Each recipe has a note on the country of origin, and a bit of a backstory for how I first came about it and why I love it.

To make the book as accessible as possible for every level of cook or simply for every mood, I have coded the recipes into time promises and complexity levels, all denoted by the symbols in the key below. By being able to choose your level and challenge yourself when you feel like it, I really hope that you'll end up loving stew just as much as I do.

KEY

 **SUPER SPEEDY** recipes take less than 45 minutes to make

 WEEKEND COOKING recipes take a bit of time to make, including marinating

 WORTH THE WAIT recipes are a bit more involved and need attention when cooking

 FLEX THE FLAVOUR recipes feature harder-to-find ingredients, so make sure you plan ahead to find these

Now the only thing left to do is to get cooking! Please do share your stew journey with me on social media, I would love to see you recreate my stews and hopefully fall in love with them as much as I do.

Happy cooking!
Xav

VEG

LENTEJAS CON CALABAZA	16
STEW LENTILS	18
CIAMBOTTA	20
KHORESH GHEYMEH	22
MISO MUSHROOM STEW	24
MISO, FENNEL AND SQUASH STEW	26
MISIR WAT	28
PUCA PICANTE	30
WAAKYE STEW	32
LOCRO DE ZAPALLO	34
OIL DOWN	36
JACKFRUIT AND TARRAGON STEW	38

SPAIN

LENTEJAS CON CALABAZA

SERVES FOUR

I've been really inspired by the way the Spanish use lentils – they are such a versatile ingredient. This dish is earthy, creamy, nutritious and filling, which is almost everything you want from a bowl of lentil stew. To finish it off, the pumpkin brings a welcome sweetness, and there is gentle spice from the cumin and paprika.

PREP 10 MINS

COOK 50 MINS

1 tbsp olive oil
1 onion, finely diced
4 garlic cloves, minced
200g dried green lentils, washed
1 tsp ground cumin
2 tsp dried oregano
2 tsp smoked paprika
1 tsp sweet paprika
1 litre vegetable stock
300g deseeded pumpkin flesh, cut into 2cm cubes
½ tsp white wine vinegar
salt
flat-leaf parsley leaves, to garnish

1. Heat up a large stew pot on a medium heat and add the olive oil. Once hot, add the onion and sauté for 5 minutes, until soft. Add the garlic, soften for 1 minute, then add the lentils, cumin, oregano and both paprikas. Toast them in the pot for 1 minute, then add the vegetable stock, mix well and bring to the boil. Reduce the heat to a simmer, cover the pot with the lid and simmer for 20 minutes, until the lentils are almost cooked through.

2. Add the pumpkin and cook for 15–20 minutes, until it is soft. The lentils should now be fully cooked, too. Add the white wine vinegar and season with salt to taste. Finish off with a sprinkle of parsley. Serve in bowls, just as it comes.

SERVES
FOUR

TRINIDAD

STEW LENTILS

Although I grew up eating a lot of lentils, they were mainly in delicious southern Asian stews and curries – it wasn't until recently that I discovered Caribbean-style lentils. Nowadays, this is one of my favourite ways to eat them, and this recipe – lentils in a fragrant, coconut-based sauce, laced with aromatic Trinidadian spices – is a regular feature in my cooking.

PREP
20 MINS

COOK
55 MINS

LENTILS
200g dried brown lentils, washed
10 pimento (allspice) berries
6 thyme sprigs
2 bay leaves

STEW
2 tsp vegetable oil
½ tsp caster sugar
1 onion, finely chopped
½ celery stick, cut into 2cm cubes
½ red pepper, deseeded and cut into 2cm cubes
½ green pepper, deseeded and cut into 2cm cubes
4 garlic cloves, minced
5g fresh ginger, peeled and minced
10 pimento (allspice) berries
½ tsp cayenne pepper
¼ tsp ground turmeric
4 tsp tomato purée
75g deseeded and peeled pumpkin, cut into 2cm cubes
75g sweet potato, peeled and cut into 2cm cubes
1 small carrot, peeled and cut into 2cm cubes
500ml vegetable stock or water (optional)
6 thyme sprigs
2 bay leaves
1 tsp dried marjoram
150ml coconut milk
salt
10g fresh parsley leaves, finely chopped
10g fresh coriander, finely chopped

1. Add the lentils to a large stew pot, then add 750ml of water. Bring the water to the boil on a high heat and, once boiling, add the pimento berries, thyme sprigs and bay leaves. Cover the pot with the lid and cook for 25 minutes, until the lentils are fully cooked through.

2. Meanwhile, start the stew, heat up another large stew pot on a medium-high heat and add the vegetable oil. Once hot, add the caster sugar and slowly stir. Keep stirring until the sugar starts to bubble and turn a dark brown but don't let it burn (about 2 minutes). Burning will cause the stew to be bitter, so if this happens, discard the caramel and start again.

3. Add the onion, celery and both peppers, then immediately season with a pinch of salt and cook for 5 minutes, until the vegetables are soft. Add the garlic and ginger and cook for 3 minutes, until fragrant. Add the pimento berries, cayenne and turmeric, cook for 1 minute, then add the tomato purée and mix well. Cook for 5 minutes, until the purée is a dark red colour, but not burnt.

4. Once your lentils are cooked, remove from the pot, drain and set them aside while you wait for the vegetables in the stew mixture to soften. Reserve the lentil cooking liquor (you'll need 500ml, if not using veg stock or water).

5. Add the pumpkin, sweet potato and carrot, mix well, then add the reserved cooking liquor or the vegetable stock or water, along with the thyme sprigs, bay leaves, marjoram and coconut milk. Bring the liquid to the boil, reduce the heat and simmer, uncovered, for 15 minutes, until the vegetables are cooked through.

6. When the vegetables are ready, add the lentils to the stew pot and simmer, uncovered, for 20 minutes, to bring the stew together and thicken it up. Sprinkle with the parsley and coriander, then serve.

ITALY

CIAMBOTTA

SERVES FOUR

Basil and tomato have to be a staple of Italian cooking and here they are reinvented as the base for a veggie stew of aubergines, potatoes and onions. Best of all, this stew is delicious hot, freshly made, and cold as a gazpacho. In summer, I'm a big fan of cooling it, then chilling it overnight in the fridge to have as a refreshing lunch the following day. It's hard to beat.

PREP 10 MINS

COOK 35 MINS

4 tbsp olive oil
2 onions, sliced
2 small potatoes, cut into 2cm cubes
1 red pepper, deseeded and cut into 3cm cubes
1 orange pepper, deseeded and cut into 3cm cubes
1 yellow pepper, deseeded and cut into 3cm cubes
250g courgette, cut into 3cm cubes
350g aubergine, cut into 3cm cubes
2 tomatoes, diced
500g passata
12 basil leaves, roughly chopped
salt

Serving suggestions
rustic or French bread, salad

1. Heat a large stew pot on a medium heat and add the olive oil. Once hot, add the onions, potatoes and a pinch of salt and sauté for 10 minutes, until very soft.

2. Add all the remaining vegetables and the tomatoes and mix well, then cover the pot with the lid, and cook on a medium heat for 5 minutes, until the veggies have released some of their moisture. Add the passata and basil leaves and mix well.

3. Pour 400ml of water into the pot, cover with the lid again and simmer for 20 minutes, until all the vegetables are cooked through and tender. Remove the lid, then taste and adjust the salt levels to finish. Serve with bread and salad.

IRAN

KHORESH GHEYMEH

SERVES FOUR

This is a vegan version of a traditional Iranian dish, and it has become my favourite way to use split peas. Saffron is one of my favourite spices – we're using saffron water here, which you can make by steeping a few strands of saffron in water (see page 211). If I ever have any saffron water left over, I store it in the fridge and drink it in the morning as a shot, for a health boost.

PREP
10 MINS

plus soaking

COOK
1 HR 15 MINS

1 tbsp vegetable oil
1 large onion, finely diced
200g aubergine, diced
1 tsp ground turmeric
2 tsp tomato purée
200g dried yellow split peas (soaked in cold water for at least 2 hours and drained)
2 tbsp Saffron Water (see page 211)
1 cinnamon stick
4 Persian dried black limes (or regular dried limes), pierced with a knife
1 litre vegetable stock
500ml peanut oil
2 Maris Piper potatoes, peeled and cut into strips for French fries
salt and black pepper

1. Heat a large stew pot on a medium-high heat and add the vegetable oil. Once hot, add the onion and sauté for 5 minutes, until soft. Add the aubergine, a pinch of salt and the turmeric and mix well.

2. Add the tomato purée and let it cook for 5 minutes, until the purée turns a dark red colour, but is not burnt. Add the split peas, saffron water, cinnamon stick, dried limes and vegetable stock. Season to taste with salt and pepper, then bring everything to a light simmer. Put the lid on the pot, adjust the heat and simmer for about 30–40 minutes, until the split peas are soft and tender.

3. Remove the lid and let the split pea stew simmer for a further 15–25 minutes, so that it thickens and comes together. Taste, then season with salt and pepper.

4. While the stew is finishing, heat the peanut oil in a deep frying pan (the oil shouldn't come more than halfway up the inside of the pan). Once hot, add the fries into the oil and deep-fry for 8 minutes, turning carefully, until golden brown and crisp all over. Serve the stew in bowls with the fries on top.

JAPAN

MISO MUSHROOM STEW

SERVES FOUR

Miso, soy, lentils and three types of mushroom – there's bags of umami in this stew. Miso is really good for your gut health, and as a result is one of my favourite ingredients. I use it on toast, with eggs, in soups and, of course, in stews. I developed this recipe for exactly that reason and the result is a simple, tasty, creamy, gut-friendly bowl of deliciousness.

PREP
10 MINS

COOK
1 HR 5 MINS

150g black lentils, washed
3 bay leaves
1 rosemary sprig
1 tbsp coconut oil
1 onion, finely diced
100g leek, finely diced
3 garlic cloves, minced
3 tsp brown miso paste
6 chestnut mushrooms, quartered
6 white mushrooms, thinly sliced
2 shiitake mushrooms, sliced (optional)
1 tbsp sweet soy sauce
400ml vegetable stock
200ml coconut milk
salt

1. Bring 800ml of water to the boil in a large stew pot on a high heat. When the water is boiling, add the lentils to the pot along with the bay leaves and rosemary. Reduce the heat and simmer with the lid off for 25 minutes, until the lentils are cooked. Drain the lentils and set them aside, discarding the herbs.

2. In a separate stew pot, heat the coconut oil on a medium-high heat. Once melted and hot, add the onion and leek and sauté for 5 minutes, until soft. Add the garlic and miso paste, mix well and soften the garlic for 2 minutes.

3. Add all the mushrooms and lightly sauté for 2 minutes, then pour in the soy sauce, vegetable stock and coconut milk, bring the liquid to the boil, then reduce the heat and cover the pot with the lid. Simmer the stew for 20 minutes, until the flavours come together nicely. Taste and adjust the salt levels, then add the cooked lentils to the pot. Leave them to simmer for 10 minutes on a medium-high heat to help thicken and reduce the stew. Serve with rice.

Serving suggestion
white rice

JAPAN

MISO, FENNEL AND SQUASH STEW

SERVES FOUR

Fennel seeds bring a delicate, earthy flavour to this wonderful stew, making it really distinctive. It took me a while to get into cooking with fennel, but now I love it. I've played around with various flavour profiles and combinations – beginning with the obvious fennel and sausage, then fennel and coconut, and then I landed on fennel and miso. It works so well.

PREP 10 MINS **COOK** 45 MINS

- 2 tbsp sunflower oil
- 2 onions, finely diced
- 2 carrots, peeled and finely diced
- 2 tsp fennel seeds
- 6 tsp white miso paste
- 4 tsp mirin
- 300g deseeded squash or pumpkin, flesh cut into 5cm cubes
- 1 x 400g can black-eye peas, drained and rinsed
- 600ml vegetable stock
- salt

1. Heat up a large stew pot on a medium heat and add the sunflower oil. Once hot, add the onions and carrots, then season with a pinch of salt and sauté for 2 minutes to begin to soften. Add the fennel seeds, reduce the heat to low and sauté for 10 minutes – low and slow until the onions and carrots are fully soft.

2. Add the miso paste, cook for 2 minutes, then add the mirin to deglaze the pot. Tip in the squash or pumpkin and black-eye peas and mix well. Add the vegetable stock, taste and season with salt to your liking. Cover the pot with the lid and simmer on a low heat for 20 minutes, until the squash/pumpkin is tender.

3. Mash about one quarter of the squash/pumpkin with the back of a fork and then leave the stew to simmer for a further 10 minutes, uncovered, until it is creamy and thick. Serve with quinoa.

Serving suggestion
quinoa

ETHIOPIA

MISIR WAT

SERVES FOUR

Berbere is a smoky, fiery spice blend popular in Ethiopian cooking and essential for this classic red lentil stew. The blend given here makes more than you need for this recipe, but you can store it and use it another time – it will keep in an airtight jar in the cupboard for 6 weeks. Niter kibbeh is a flavoured, clarified butter – like a spiced ghee. It's really simple to make and, although it's optional in the recipe, any effort is well worth it.

PREP
15 MINS

COOK
50 MINS

2 tbsp ghee
3 red onions, finely diced
2 tbsp berbere (see below)
2 tbsp niter kibbeh (optional; see below)
200g chopped fresh or canned tomatoes
100g dried whole red lentils, rinsed
500ml vegetable stock
salt

BERBERE (makes 5 tablespoons)
1 tbsp black peppercorns
1½ tsp cumin seeds
½ tsp coriander seeds
½ tsp fenugreek seeds
3 cloves
5 pimento (allspice) berries
4 dried bird's eye chillies, deseeded and roughly chopped
5 green cardamom pods
½ tsp ground turmeric
¼ tsp ground nutmeg
½ tsp ground cinnamon
2 tsp smoked paprika

NITER KIBBEH (SPICED BUTTER)
200g salted butter
1 cinnamon stick
1 black cardamom pod
1 tsp black peppercorns
2 tsp coriander seeds
2 cloves
½ onion, quartered
1 tsp garlic paste
1½ tsp ginger paste
½ tsp ground turmeric
1 tsp dried oregano
½ tsp ground nutmeg

Serving suggestion
Ethiopian injera bread or rice.

1. Make the berbere. Put a dry frying pan on a medium-high heat and add the peppercorns, cumin seeds, coriander seeds, fenugreek seeds, cloves and pimento berries. Toast for 30 seconds until fragrant, then immediately remove them from the pan on to a plate. Leave them to cool completely, then transfer them to a spice grinder or into a mortar and add all the remaining berbere ingredients. Grind until the blend is as smooth and fine as you can make it. (You'll have more than you need – see the recipe intro for storage info.)

2. Make the niter kibbeh (if using). Put a large saucepan on a medium heat. Add the butter, then once melted, add all the remaining ingredients and mix well. Turn the heat down and let it simmer for 1 hour, until the flavours have infused. Place a sieve over a heatproof bowl and strain the butter into the bowl, then use straight away or cool and store in an airtight jar in the fridge for up to 3 weeks.

3. To make the stew, heat up a large stew pot on a medium heat and add the ghee. Once melted and hot, add the onions and reduce the heat to low. Cover the pot with the lid and leave the onions to cook, low and slow, for about 20 minutes, until deeply caramelised and soft.

4. Add 2 tablespoons of the berbere (or more or less, depending on your preference for heat) and mix well. Cover with the lid again and cook for 5 minutes, until aromatic.

5. Add the niter kibbeh (if using) and mix well, then add the chopped tomatoes. Stir, then cover the pot again and cook for 5 minutes, until the tomatoes have broken down.

6. Add the lentils and vegetable stock, then season to taste with salt. Put the lid on again and simmer for 20 minutes, until the lentils are cooked. Serve with Ethiopian injera bread or rice.

PERU

PUCA PICANTE

SERVES FOUR

This is a Peruvian, beetroot-based stew – the name literally means 'spicy red' – that in a non-veggie version might have various meats, usually pork, added. However, I think it's delicious just as it is – infused with cumin, coriander, and oregano, then finished off with creamy white beans to give texture in place of the meat. For me, beetroot is one of the most under-appreciated vegetables in the world. Here it develops a natural sweetness that helps to balance out the heat from the aji panca.

PREP 15 MINS

COOK 45 MINS

1 tbsp olive oil
1 large red onion, finely diced
6 garlic cloves, minced
6 tbsp aji panca paste (available online or in South American shops)
1 tsp ground cumin
2 tsp ground coriander
1½ tsp dried Mexican oregano (or regular oregano)
500g raw beetroots, peeled and diced into 2.5cm cubes
300ml vegetable stock
120g shelled raw, unsalted peanuts
1 x 400g can cannellini beans, drained and rinsed
2 limes, juiced
salt

Serving suggestions
white rice, sliced raw red onion

1. Put a large stew pot on a medium heat and add the olive oil. Once hot, add the onion and sauté for 5 minutes, until soft. Add the garlic and soften for 1 minute, stirring occasionally, then add the aji panca paste and cook for 4 minutes, until thickened.

2. Season with the cumin, coriander and oregano, mix well and cook for 5 minutes to cook out the spices. Add the beetroot and vegetable stock and bring everything to a light simmer. Cover the pot with the lid, reduce the heat and simmer for 20 minutes, until the beetroot is cooked through.

3. Meanwhile, heat a small, non-stick frying pan on a medium-high heat. Add the peanuts and lightly toast for 2–3 minutes, until fragrant. Remove the nuts from the pan to stop them burning and set them aside.

4. Once the beetroot is cooked, remove about one quarter of it from the pot and tip it into a blender with the toasted peanuts and the beans. Blitz until smooth. Add this mixture back to the stew and mix well. Simmer, uncovered, for 10 minutes, until thickened. Squeeze over the lime juice, mix well, season to taste with salt, then serve with rice and topped with raw red onion.

GHANA

SERVES FOUR

WAAKYE STEW

This is my version of Ghana's take on rice and beans, which I've made more substantial by adding tender mushrooms (in Ghana, it may be served as an accompaniment to various dishes, including meat ones). The star of this dish is definitely the mushroom broth, which is beautifully rich and warming.

PREP
20 MINS

COOK
1 HR 5 MINS

TOMATO MIXTURE
2 large tomatoes, halved
1 red pepper, deseeded and halved
1 Romano pepper, deseeded and halved
2 red onions, quartered
10 garlic cloves, peeled but left whole

MUSHROOM BROTH
(makes about 750ml)
1 vegetable stock cube
1 rosemary sprig
1 star anise
½ tsp ground cumin
½ tsp ground ginger
½ tsp ground coriander
1 tsp mixed peppercorns
4 cloves
2 bay leaves
4 king oyster mushrooms, halved
2 shiitake mushrooms, halved
2 chestnut mushrooms, halved
salt and black pepper

STEW
2 tbsp sunflower oil
2 tbsp red pepper paste
2 tbsp tomato purée
1 tbsp garlic paste
2 star anise
½ tsp ground nutmeg
2 bay leaves

Serving suggestions
Waakye Rice (see page 207) and soft-boiled eggs, peeled and halved

1. Preheat the oven to 240°C/220°C fan. Place all the ingredients for the tomato mixture in a large ovenproof dish, and roast them for 20 minutes, until soft. Set aside.

2. In the meantime, pour 750ml of water into a large stew pot and place it on a high heat. Once boiling, add all the ingredients for the mushroom broth, apart from the mushrooms, and mix well. Cover the pot with the lid, reduce the heat and simmer for 10 minutes, until the water is infused with the spices. Taste and season with salt, then add all the mushrooms. Simmer for 20 minutes with the lid on, until the mushrooms are tender and the flavours have come together. Then, scoop out the mushrooms, squeezing out all the juices back into the pot, pat them dry and set aside for the stew. Strain the mushroom cooking water into a jug and measure out 400ml (discard the contents of the sieve). This is your mushroom broth. Set it aside and store the remainder in an airtight jar in the fridge for up to 10 days.

3. Tip the roasted tomatoes and vegetables into a blender or food processor and blitz to a paste. Set aside.

4. Heat up a large stew pot on a medium heat and add the sunflower oil. Once hot, add the reserved mushrooms and sear them for 2 minutes, turning, until they are nicely golden all over. Remove the mushrooms from the pot and set aside. Add the red pepper paste, tomato purée and garlic paste to the pot, then cook for 2 minutes, until aromatic.

5. Add the blended tomato and vegetable mixture to the pot and cook for 5 minutes, until aromatic. Add the reserved 400ml of mushroom broth, along with the star anise, nutmeg and bay leaves. Season with salt and pepper to taste. Bring the liquid to the boil, add the mushrooms back to the pot, then reduce the heat and simmer, uncovered, for 25 minutes, to allow the flavours to infuse and the stew to reduce and thicken nicely. Serve with the Waakye Rice and boiled egg halves.

PERU

LOCRO DE ZAPALLO

SERVES FOUR

This warming and creamy squash-based stew embodies the richness of Andean cuisine. I have only recently started to introduce hominy (dried and treated corn) into my cooking. I first tried it with a Mexican pozole, a corn-based soup, and I loved the texture. With a bit of digging, I stumbled on this traditional Peruvian dish and fell in love with the combination. The corn gives a soft, yet chewy texture and is great for soaking up all the other flavours. Queso fresco is a Latin American fresh cheese that's similar to halloumi, but far milder and creamier in flavour. It may be served crumbled or cubed to sprinkle over the stew at the end, but instead I'm incorporating it for extra creaminess.

PREP 15 MINS
plus overnight soaking

COOK 40 MINS

- 1 tbsp sunflower oil
- 1 large red onion, finely diced
- 6 tbsp aji amarillo paste
- 4 garlic cloves, minced
- 2 tsp ground cumin
- 500g squash, peeled, deseeded and chopped into small cubes
- 600ml vegetable stock or water
- 20g fresh coriander or huacatay (leaves and stems)
- 100g dried Mexican hominy, soaked overnight in water, then drained
- 50g queso fresco (or feta cheese)
- 2 tbsp evaporated milk
- salt and black pepper

1. Heat a large stew pot on a medium heat and add the sunflower oil. Once hot, add the onion and sauté for 5 minutes, until soft. Add the aji amarillo paste and garlic and cook for 2 minutes, until the garlic is soft and the paste thickened. Add the ground cumin and mix well.

2. Tip in the squash, mix very well, then pour in the vegetable stock or water. Add the coriander or huacatay. Season to taste with salt and pepper, then bring the liquid to the boil. Cover the pot with the lid, reduce the heat and simmer the stew for 15 minutes, until the squash is tender.

3. Add the hominy to the pot and cook for 10 minutes. Remove the coriander or huacatay stems, then season to taste again with salt. Finally, add the queso fresco and the evaporated milk. Mix well, then cook for 5 minutes, until the cheese has melted and incorporated into the stew. Serve with rice, lime wedges and fresh coriander leaves, and topped with a fried egg if you like.

Serving suggestions
white rice, lime wedges, fresh coriander leaves, fried eggs

CARIBBEAN

OIL DOWN

SERVES FOUR

Oil down is more than just a dish – it's a Caribbean symbol of family, neighbours and tradition. In Grenada, where it is the national dish, it's often eaten at events and gatherings. The traditional version contains far more than this recipe, with ingredients such as salted meat, chicken and cassava. I decided I wanted to do a plant-based alternative. The starchy vegetables work really well – they absorb all that wonderful flavour from the sauce, as well as providing great texture.

PREP 20 MINS

COOK 35 MINS

1 tsp ground turmeric
3 tbsp Saffron Water (see page 211)
400ml coconut milk
1 tbsp coconut oil
1 onion, finely diced
5g fresh ginger, peeled and finely diced
3 garlic cloves, minced
2½ tbsp Green Seasoning (see page 210)
200g breadfruit, quartered, then thinly sliced lengthways
100g deseeded squash or pumpkin flesh, cut into 1–2cm cubes
½ carrot, peeled and cut into 1cm discs
60g flat or runner beans, chopped into 3cm chunks
1 green banana, peeled and cut into 1cm discs
200g canned callaloo (drained weight)
salt and black pepper

SPINNERS
50g plain flour

Serving suggestions
white rice, lime wedges, fresh coriander

1 In a large bowl, mix together the turmeric, saffron water, coconut milk and 200ml of water. Season to taste with salt and pepper, then set aside.

2 Heat up a large stew pot on a medium heat and add the coconut oil. Once melted and hot, add the onion and sauté for 5 minutes, until soft. Add the ginger, garlic and green seasoning, mix well and soften for 1 minute.

3 Now start layering with the breadfruit, then the squash or pumpkin, carrot, runner beans and banana on top of the onion. Pour over the coconut milk mixture and bring the liquid to a light simmer. Cover the pot with the lid, reduce the heat and simmer for 20 minutes, until the coconut milk starts to bubble away and a fragrant sauce begins to develop.

4 Meanwhile, make the spinners. Tip the flour into a mixing bowl, season with a pinch of salt and mix the flour and salt together with your hands. Add 2 tablespoons of cold water and bring the mixture together to form a dough. Knead the dough for 2 minutes to develop the gluten, then cover the bowl with a clean tea towel, and leave the dough to rest for 10 minutes.

5 Once the dough is rested, break off small pieces (each about the size of a small ball is enough) and roll ('spin', hence the name) each between your palms to form a long, thin cylinder. You should get about 5 spinners in total. Add these to the pot along with the callaloo, then simmer with the lid on for 10 minutes, until the spinners are cooked through and the stew is piping hot. Serve with rice, lime wedges and fresh coriander.

GEORGIAN AND PERSIAN-INSPIRED

JACKFRUIT AND TARRAGON STEW

SERVES FOUR

Pieces of tender jackfruit are simmered in an aromatic white wine and tarragon-based broth, infused with tangy dried limes and ground turmeric, then finished off with creamy adzuki beans. Tarragon is a truly wonderful ingredient, slightly sweet and citrusy with a subtle anise-like flavour! Paired with the sweetness from the white wine and tanginess from the dried limes it creates a delicious bold flavour!

PREP
10 MINS

COOK
1 HR 15 MINS

1 tbsp olive oil
2 large shallots, finely diced
6 garlic cloves, minced
3 tsp ground turmeric
100g tarragon, leaves picked and finely chopped
50g fresh coriander, finely chopped
300ml white wine
500g canned jackfruit in brine, drained and rinsed, then shredded
1 litre vegetable stock
4 Persian dried black limes, pierced with a knife
1 x 400g can adzuki beans, drained and rinsed
salt and black pepper

1. Heat a large stew pot on a medium heat and add the olive oil. Add the shallots with a pinch of salt and sauté for 5 minutes, until soft. Add the garlic, soften for 1 minute, then add the turmeric. Cook for 5 minutes on a medium-low heat to cook out the spice.

2. Add the tarragon and coriander and sauté for 1 minute. Add the white wine to deglaze the pot, then leave to bubble away until reduced by half (about 10 minutes). Add the shredded jackfruit, then the vegetable stock and dried limes. Bring the liquid to a simmer, cover the pot with the lid, and simmer for 20 minutes, until the flavours are well incorporated.

3. Season to taste with salt and pepper, then add the adzuki beans. Mix well, cover the pot with the lid again and simmer for 20 minutes, until the flavours have fully come together and the jackfruit is tender. Remove the lid and leave the stew to reduce for 10–15 minutes, until thick. Serve with rice.

Serving suggestion
white rice

BEANS

QORMA A LUBIA	42
LOUBIA	44
CHICKPEA MAAFE	46
GARBANZOS ESPAÑOL	48
STEW PEAS	50
RED BEANS	52
CHICKPEA MASALA	54
DAUBE	56
HARISSA BLACK-EYE PEAS	58
ITAL STEW	60
FASOLIA	62

AFGHANISTAN

QORMA A LUBIA

SERVES FOUR

This kidney bean stew celebrates the rich flavours of Afghan cuisine – it is a perfect stew if you're looking for only a few steps and readily available ingredients without compromising on flavour. Light, but wholesome, this is one deeply satisfying dish!

PREP 10 MINS
COOK 35 MINS

3 tbsp olive oil
2 onions, finely diced
1 tsp ground turmeric
1 tsp ground black pepper
20g fresh ginger, peeled and minced
8 garlic cloves, minced
4 tbsp tomato purée
500g passata
300ml vegetable stock
2 x 400g cans red kidney beans, drained and rinsed
5g mint leaves, finely chopped
10g fresh coriander, leaves picked and chopped
salt

1. Heat up a large stew pot on a medium heat and add the olive oil. Once hot, add the onion and season with salt. Sauté for 2 minutes, until the onion softens a little. Add the turmeric and black pepper and cook for 5 minutes, until the onion is very soft and the spices are cooked out. Add the ginger and garlic, soften for 1 minute, then add the tomato purée and cook for 5 minutes, until the purée is a dark red colour, but is not burnt.

2. Pour in the passata and vegetable stock, then add the kidney beans, mix well and bring the liquid to the boil. Reduce the heat to a simmer, cover the pot with the lid and simmer for 15 minutes, until everything is cooked through.

3. Remove the lid and let the stew cook, uncovered, for a further 5 minutes, to thicken. At the end, add the mint and coriander, then season to taste with salt. Serve with flatbreads and salad.

Serving suggestions
chapatis or other flatbreads, salad

MOROCCO

LOUBIA

SERVES FOUR

An iconic and beloved Moroccan household staple, this stew comprises tender cannellini beans simmered down in a rich tomato-based sauce, infused with turmeric, coriander and cumin. I'll never forget making this dish in Morocco. Sam, my amazing videographer, and I drove up into the stunning Atlas mountains to a place called Todra Gorge. We climbed a mountain and set up our equipment (including my gas stove from home) and filmed this for my Beans from Around the World series. There's something really special about making and eating fresh food in nature – with great company!

PREP
5 MINS

COOK
40 MINS

2 tbsp olive oil
2 large onions, grated
6 garlic cloves, minced
6 tbsp tomato purée
4 tsp smoked paprika
4 tsp ground cumin
1 tsp ground ginger
4 tsp ground turmeric
1 tsp ground coriander
½ tsp cayenne pepper
1 tsp ground cardamom
400g passata
300ml vegetable stock
20g flat-leaf parsley, leaves picked and finely chopped
20g fresh coriander, leaves picked and finely chopped
2 x 400g cans cannellini beans, drained and rinsed
salt and sugar, to taste

Serving suggestion
bread

1. Heat up a large stew pot or hob-safe tagine on a medium heat and add the olive oil. Once hot, add the onions and sauté for 3 minutes to soften a little. Add the garlic and tomato purée, then cook for 5 minutes, until the purée turns a dark red colour, but is not burnt. Add half of each spice, then mix well and cook for a further 2 minutes.

2. Add the passata, vegetable stock, the remaining spices and half each of the chopped parsley and coriander, then mix well and bring to the boil. Reduce the heat to a simmer, cover the pot or tagine with the lid and simmer for 20 minutes, until the flavours have thoroughly developed.

3. Add the cannellini beans, season to taste with salt and sugar, then simmer, uncovered, for a further 10 minutes, until the beans are heated through. Serve with bread.

WEST AFRICA

CHICKPEA MAAFE

SERVES FOUR

This stew is a plant-based delight. I grew up eating a lot of chickpeas, because my mother absolutely loved them. If I'm completely honest, though, I wasn't a big fan – until recently. This recipe changed how I view humble chickpeas and is now one of my go-to ways to eat them. They add a wonderful, earthy element that goes so well with the rich, creamy peanut flavour. There is a bold range of spices here, too. It's a real treat!

PREP
15 MINS

COOK
40 MINS

60g smooth peanut butter
100ml boiling water
2 tbsp peanut oil
1 onion, diced
½ green pepper, deseeded and diced
1½ tsp cumin seeds
½ tsp ground turmeric
4 garlic cloves, minced
150g aubergine, cut into small dice
200g deseeded squash flesh, cubed
120g sweet potato, peeled and cubed
2 tbsp tomato purée
½ tsp ground ginger
2 tsp ground cardamom
¼ tsp cayenne pepper
1 tsp ground cumin
2 x 400g cans chickpeas, drained and rinsed
6 thyme sprigs
2 bay leaves
700ml vegetable stock or water
20g fresh coriander, leaves picked and chopped
salt

Serving suggestion
white rice

1. In a large bowl, combine the peanut butter with the boiling water and whisk until smooth, then set aside.

2. Heat up a large stew pot on a medium heat and add the peanut oil. Once hot, add the onion and green pepper and cook for 2 minutes. Add the cumin seeds and cook for 5 minutes, until the onion and pepper are soft and fragrant. Add the turmeric and cook for 3 minutes, until aromatic.

3. Add the garlic, sauté for 1 minute, then add the aubergine, squash and sweet potato. Cook for 2 minutes, then add the tomato purée and cook for a further 3 minutes, until the purée turns a dark red colour, but is not burnt.

4. Add the ground spices, along with the chickpeas, thyme, bay leaves and vegetable stock or water. Bring the liquid to the boil, then reduce the heat, cover the pot with the lid, and simmer for 15 minutes, to let the flavours come together.

5. Remove the lid, add your peanut butter mixture, then mix very well. Season to taste with salt, then simmer, uncovered, for 10 minutes, until the peanut butter mixture is cooked through. Finish with the chopped coriander and extra salt to taste, and serve with rice.

SPAIN

GARBANZOS ESPAÑOL

SERVES FOUR

This robust Spanish stew involves simmering down chickpeas in a smoky tomato- and chorizo-based sauce infused with Spanish paprika and rosemary. For me, though, the stars of this stew are the blitzed toasted bread and garlic that you add at the end – rustic Spanish home-cooking if ever there was. It's a versatile stew, too – for example, you can easily make it veggie by removing the chorizo, if you like.

PREP 10 MINS

COOK 35 MINS

- 2 tbsp olive oil, plus 1 tsp for the baguette
- 1 tsp cumin seeds
- 120g cooking chorizo, sliced
- 1 onion, diced
- 1 red pepper, deseeded and diced
- 2 tbsp tomato purée
- 2 Roma tomatoes, grated
- 2 tsp sweet paprika
- 1 tsp smoked paprika
- 2 bay leaves
- 1 small rosemary sprig
- 2 x 400g cans chickpeas, drained and rinsed
- 500ml vegetable stock or water
- 160g baby spinach
- 40g baguette, sliced
- 2 garlic cloves, thinly sliced
- salt

1. Heat up a large stew pot on a medium heat and add the olive oil. Once hot, add the cumin seeds and lightly toast until fragrant (about 30 seconds). Add the chorizo and let some of the fat render, then add the onion and red pepper and cook for 5 minutes, until soft. Add the tomato purée and cook on a medium heat for 5 minutes, until it is a dark red colour, but is not burnt.

2. Add the tomatoes, both paprikas, the bay leaves and rosemary and mix well. Then, add the chickpeas and cook for 2 minutes. Add the vegetable stock or water, bring the liquid to the boil, then reduce the heat to a simmer, cover the pot with the lid and simmer for 15 minutes, until the flavours have come together.

3. Add the spinach leaves, re-cover the pot and leave the spinach to wilt fully for about 5 minutes on a medium heat.

4. In the meantime, heat up a large skillet on a medium heat. Add the teaspoon of olive oil, then once hot, add the baguette slices and toast them on both sides until almost burnt (about 2 minutes each side). Remove the baguette slices, add the garlic and lightly toast it for 30 seconds (make sure it doesn't burn).

5. Add the toasted bread and garlic to a food processor and blend until smooth. Add this mixture to the stew and mix very well to fully incorporate. Remove the rosemary sprig and let the stew simmer for a few minutes to heat through. Taste and adjust the salt levels, and you're ready to go.

JAMAICA

STEW PEAS

SERVES FOUR

My version of this Jamaican staple involves soaking red kidney beans overnight, then slow-cooking them the next day in an aromatic coconut- and thyme-based broth, infused with bold Caribbean spices. I'll never forget the first time I ate this in Jamaica. I was in a downtown Ital restaurant in Kingston, with a few friends. Oh. My. Word. I dream about the bowl of stew peas in our order to this day. I believe it's the combination of tasty Jamaican produce and years of craft that made it so special – my taste buds were truly blessed. I can't seem to replicate the exact experience, but this is pretty close.

PREP
20 MINS

plus overnight soaking

COOK
2 HRS 10 MINS

2 tbsp coconut oil
1 red onion, finely diced
1 large spring onion, finely diced
10g fresh ginger, peeled and minced
6 garlic cloves, minced
200g dried red kidney beans, soaked overnight in water, then drained and rinsed
2 tbsp pimento (allspice) berries
6 cloves
2 tbsp ground black pepper
4 bay leaves
10 thyme sprigs or 2 tbsp dried thyme
1.4 litres boiling water
300ml coconut milk
½ tsp cayenne pepper
150g sweet potato, peeled and cut into 3cm cubes
150g pumpkin or butternut squash, peeled, deseeded and cut into 3cm cubes
150g cassava, peeled and cut into 3cm cubes
¼ tsp salt, plus extra to season
100g plain flour

1. Heat up a large stew pot on a medium heat and add the coconut oil. Once melted and hot, add the red onion, spring onion, ginger and garlic and cook for 5 minutes, until soft. Add the rehydrated kidney beans, the pimento berries, cloves, black pepper, bay leaves, thyme and boiling water. Bring the liquid to the boil, then reduce the heat, put the lid on the pot and simmer for 1 hour, until the beans are soft and the liquid is a dark red colour.

2. Add the coconut milk and cayenne pepper and season with salt to taste. Add the sweet potato, pumpkin or squash and cassava, part-cover the pot with the lid and simmer for 20 minutes, until the vegetables are tender. Have a taste, you can remove the pimento berries at this point should you choose to.

3. Meanwhile, mix together the ¼ teaspoon of salt and the flour in a large bowl. Little by little, add enough water to bring the flour together into a dough (you'll need about 4 tablespoons of water). Knead the dough in the bowl for 2 minutes, then cover the bowl with a clean tea towel and leave the dough to rest for 5 minutes.

4. Divide the rested dough into 8 equal-sized pieces and roll each piece between your palms into a ball and then into a cylinder (gently pinch the ends and roll to form a point). Add the cylindrical dough pieces into the stew, part-cover with the lid again and simmer everything together for 15 minutes. Remove the lid completely and simmer for a further 30 minutes, until the stew has reduced to a nice, thick consistency and the dumplings are cooked.

5. Remove the pot from the heat and use the back of a fork to mash about one third of the kidney beans in the mixture, to thicken up the stew even more. Serve with Jamaican Rice and Peas, and fried plantain slices.

Serving suggestions
Rice and Peas (see page 202), fried plantain slices

GHANA

RED BEANS

SERVES FOUR

Embrace the bold flavours of West Africa with my plant-based version of the classic Ghanaian Red Red – pure comfort food that's great on its own or as part of a larger feast. It's a statement to simplicity and a regular in my kitchen. I have made it with and without palm oil and I've found that the palm oil is the thing that makes all the difference, providing that iconic savoury and earthy West African flavour. It is worth noting that traditionally this stew is cooked with smoked and salted fish, as well as other beloved Ghanaian ingredients, but I decided to simplify it and give you a plant-based version.

PREP
10 MINS

COOK
30 MINS

3 tbsp sustainable palm oil
1 onion, sliced
4 garlic cloves, minced
12g fresh ginger, peeled and finely chopped
160g cherry tomatoes, halved
100g passata
½ tsp ground cumin
1 tsp smoked paprika
¼ tsp cayenne pepper
2 x 400g cans black-eye peas, drained and rinsed
salt

1. Heat up a large stew pot on a medium heat and add the palm oil. Once hot, add the onion and sauté for 5 minutes, until soft. Add the garlic and ginger and soften for 1 minute.

2. Add the cherry tomatoes and mix well. Cover the pot with the lid, reduce the heat to medium-low and cook for a few more minutes, until the tomatoes have broken down. Remove the lid and add the passata, 300ml of water and the spices and mix well. Cover the pot again and cook for 10 minutes, until everything has come together.

3. Add the black-eye peas, mix very well, then taste and adjust the salt levels to your preference. Simmer, uncovered, for a further 10 minutes, then serve with rice, fried plantain slices and mashed avocado, and enjoy!

Serving suggestions
rice, fried plantain, mashed avocado

SERVES FOUR

INDIA

CHICKPEA MASALA

Inspired by the wonderfully diverse flavours of India, this chickpea masala embraces the perfect combination of spice and comfort. I visited India in 2014 and I'll never forget how incredible the vegetarian food was. The inspiration for this dish came from something in Udaipur – I can't remember the name of it, but I do distinctly remember the flavour. It had tender chickpeas in a lovely coconut sauce – just like this version, developed ten years later.

PREP
15 MINS

COOK
45 MINS

1 tsp coconut oil
¼ tsp coriander seeds
½ tsp cumin seeds
⅛ tsp yellow mustard seeds
1 red onion, sliced
5g fresh ginger, peeled and finely chopped
3 garlic cloves, minced
1 small tomato, diced
2 bay leaves
5 fresh curry leaves (or use dried, if necessary)
½ tsp curry powder
¼ tsp red chilli powder
1 tbsp tomato purée
1 x 400g can chickpeas, drained and rinsed
50g peeled and deseeded squash or pumpkin, cut into 2cm cubes
100ml coconut milk
250ml vegetable stock
½ tsp garam masala
½ lime, juiced
5g fresh coriander, leaves picked and chopped
salt

1 Heat a stew pot on a medium heat and add the coconut oil. Once melted and hot, add the coriander, cumin and mustard seeds and fry for 20–30 seconds, until fragrant. Add the onion, ginger and garlic, mix well and sauté for 5 minutes, until soft. Add the diced tomato, bay leaves and curry leaves, mix well and cook for 2 minutes, until fragrant.

2 Add the curry powder and red chilli powder and stir over the heat for 2 minutes. Add the tomato purée, increase the heat and cook for 5 minutes, until the purée turns a dark red colour, but is not burnt. Add in the chickpeas and squash or pumpkin, then mix very well so that everything is fully combined.

3 Pour in the coconut milk and vegetable stock, mix well again and bring the liquid to the boil. Reduce the heat, cover the pot with the lid and simmer for 20 minutes, until the flavours have really come together.

4 Remove the lid from the pot and leave the stew to thicken up for a further 10 minutes. Add the garam masala, then taste and season with salt to taste. Turn off the heat, then stir through the lime juice and sprinkle over the chopped coriander to finish. Serve with Indian flatbreads, such as chapatis or naan breads.

Serving suggestions
chapatis or naan breads

MAURITIUS

DAUBE

SERVES FOUR

Experience the flavours of the Indian Ocean with a trip to the tropical island of Mauritius! I didn't know much about Mauritian cuisine until I started working on this book, and now I'm fascinated by it. It's a wonderful blend of Indian, Chinese, European and African influences. This is my vegetarian version of the traditional Mauritian chicken daube – soft red kidney beans are simmered in a tomato-based sauce infused with cardamom, cinnamon and cloves.

PREP
15 MINS

COOK
40 MINS

1 tbsp coconut oil
1 red onion, sliced
1 cinnamon stick
2 green cardamom pods
½ tsp cumin seeds
5 cloves
6 fresh or dried curry leaves
3 garlic cloves, minced
5g fresh ginger, peeled and finely chopped
100g aubergine, cut into 3cm cubes
1 tbsp tomato purée
100g passata
300ml vegetable stock
1 tsp dried thyme
150g sweet potato, peeled and cut into 3cm cubes
1 carrot, peeled and cut into 3cm cubes
1 x 400g can red kidney beans, drained and rinsed
50g frozen peas
10g fresh coriander leaves, chopped
salt and black pepper

Serving suggestion
white rice

1. Heat up a large stew pot on a medium heat and add the coconut oil. Once melted and hot, add the onion and a pinch of salt and sauté for 1 minute to just soften. Add the cinnamon stick, cardamom pods, cumin seeds, cloves and curry leaves and leave them to cook for 5 minutes, until aromatic.

2. Add your garlic and ginger and cook for 1 minute to soften. Add the aubergine and cook for 2 minutes, until soft, then add the tomato purée and fry it for 5 minutes, until the purée turns a dark red colour, but is not burnt.

3. Pour in the passata and vegetable stock, add the thyme, sweet potato, carrot and kidney beans, then mix well. Bring the liquid to the boil and season to taste with salt and pepper. Cover the pot with the lid, reduce the heat and simmer for 20 minutes, until the vegetables are tender. Adjust the seasoning to taste.

4. Add the frozen peas and simmer, uncovered, for 2 minutes, until heated through. Sprinkle with the chopped coriander to finish and serve with rice.

NORTH AFRICA

HARISSA BLACK-EYE PEAS

SERVES FOUR

Harissa is a fiery and delicious chilli paste originating from Tunisia and used throughout the Maghreb region of northern Africa. It can spice up tagines, complete marinades and level-up sauces – it's a store-cupboard essential for me. I came up with this stew almost by accident: I was making a simple harissa and black-eye stew and added a dash too much harissa. So, to combat the heat, I added some cream and was really impressed with the result. Another one for the book!

PREP
10 MINS

COOK
40 MINS

2 tbsp olive oil
½ tsp coriander seeds
½ tsp cumin seeds
2 tsp Ras el Hanout (see page 209)
1 red onion, finely diced
5 garlic cloves, minced
8 tsp harissa paste
4 tsp tomato purée
1 preserved lemon, drained, skin finely shredded, and pulp (with pips removed)
2 tbsp juice from the preserved lemon jar
250ml vegetable stock
1 x 400g can black-eye peas, drained and rinsed
50ml single cream
25g flat-leaf parsley leaves and stems, finely chopped
25g fresh coriander leaves and stems, finely chopped
salt and pepper

Serving suggestion
white rice

1. Heat up a large stew pot or hob-safe tagine on a medium heat and add the olive oil. Once hot, add the coriander seeds, cumin seeds and half the ras el hanout. Fry them for 30 seconds, until fragrant. Add the onion and sauté for 5 minutes, until soft, then add the garlic and soften for 1 minute.

2. Add the harissa paste and tomato purée to the pot and cook for 2 minutes, until fragrant and darkened. Add the preserved lemon skin and pulp, the juice from the preserved lemon jar, the vegetable stock and the remaining ras el hanout, then bring the liquid to the boil. Reduce the heat, put the lid on the pot or tagine and leave the stew to simmer for 20 minutes, until the flavours come together.

3. Add the black-eye peas and simmer, uncovered, for 10 minutes to heat through. Finally, add the cream, parsley and coriander, then mix very well and season to taste with salt and pepper. Serve with rice.

CARIBBEAN

ITAL STEW

SERVES
FOUR

24 HRS

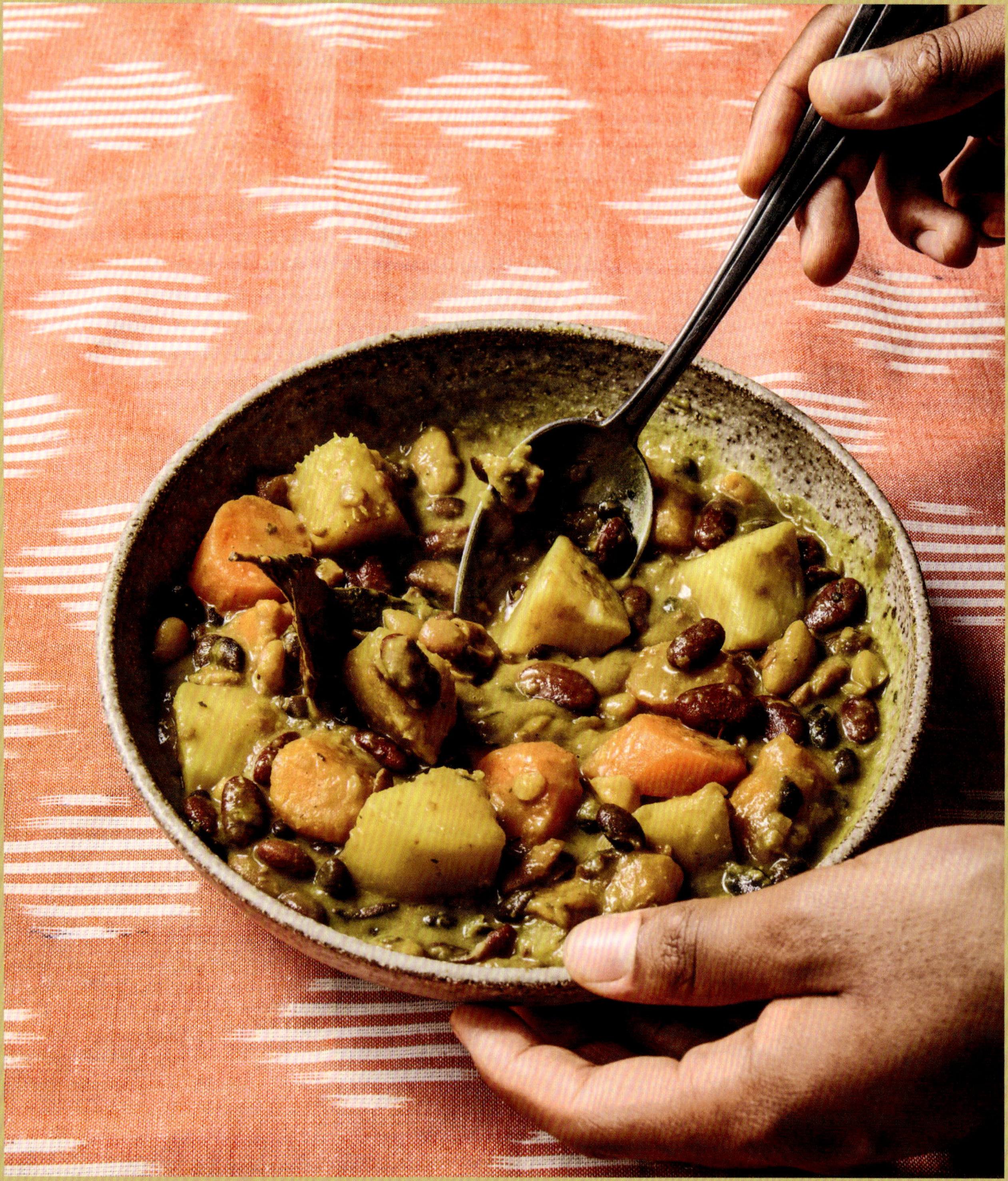

The Ital community in Jamaica is a group of people who embrace plant-based living and eating. The famous Ital stew is known for its wonderful flavours and nutritional benefits. I developed my version during my obsessive bean phase (which, for that matter, is still ongoing). For this dish, I bought a load of dried beans at a market in Portugal, soaked them overnight, then started to play around with the flavour of the stew. I tried different spice combinations and different types of bean until I found my favourites. This is the result.

PREP
20 MINS

plus overnight soaking

COOK
2 HRS 25 MINS

50g dried white haricot beans
50g dried red kidney beans
50g dried black beans
50g dried pinto beans
2 tbsp coconut oil
1 onion, finely diced
1 cinnamon stick
8 cloves
12 pimento (allspice) berries
15g fresh ginger, peeled and minced
5 garlic cloves, minced
1½ tsp ground turmeric
1 litre vegetable stock
8 thyme sprigs
1 rosemary sprig, leaves picked and finely chopped
2 bay leaves
2 tsp mixed peppercorns
300ml coconut milk
80g squash, peeled, deseeded and cut into 2cm cubes
80g cassava, peeled and cut into 2cm cubes
80g carrots, peeled and cut into 2cm cubes
80g potato, peeled and cut into 2cm cubes
80g sweet potato, peeled and cut into 2cm cubes
salt and black pepper

Serving suggestion
white rice

1. Place all your dried beans in a single, large bowl and cover them completely with cold water. Leave them to soak overnight. When you're ready to cook them, drain the beans and rinse them under cold running water for 30 seconds, then you're ready to go.

2. Heat up a large stew pot on a medium heat and add the coconut oil. Once melted and hot, add the onion and a pinch of salt. Sauté for 2 minutes, then add your cinnamon stick, cloves and pimento berries. Sauté for 5 minutes, until aromatic.

3. Add the ginger and garlic, sauté for 1 minute, then add the turmeric. Reduce the heat to low and cook for 5 minutes, until the ginger and garlic are soft and the turmeric is cooked out.

4. Add the vegetable stock, thyme, rosemary, bay leaves and mixed peppercorns to the pot, then increase the heat to bring the liquid to a light simmer. Add the soaked and rinsed beans, cover the pot with the lid, reduce the heat again and simmer for 1 hour 30 minutes, until the beans are soft and fully cooked.

5. Add the coconut milk and diced vegetables and simmer for 40 minutes with the lid partially on, until the vegetables are cooked through. Season to taste with salt and pepper, then serve with rice.

LEBANON

FASOLIA

SERVES
FOUR

Experience the flavours of Lebanon with this traditional white bean and beef stew. The combination of beans and meat in a stew gives a rich, earthy, umami flavour, and you get a great fibre/protein combination that, for a gym-lover like me, makes the perfect post-workout meal.

PREP
10 MINS

COOK
1 HR 40 MINS

2 tbsp olive oil
1kg beef shin, cut into 5cm cubes
2 tsp cumin seeds
1 tsp coriander seeds
2 onions, diced
8 garlic cloves, minced
3 tbsp Lebanese 7-spice (see page 208)
4 tbsp tomato purée
600ml beef stock
200g passata
4 cloves
1 x 400g can cannellini beans, drained and rinsed
20g fresh coriander, leaves and stems finely chopped
salt

1. Heat up a large stew pot on a medium-high heat and add the olive oil. Once hot, add your cubes of beef and sear, turning for 5 minutes, until brown all over (do this in batches, if necessary). Remove the beef from the pot and set aside.

2. Reduce to a medium heat and add the cumin and coriander seeds to the pot. Toast them for 30 seconds, until fragrant. Add the onions and garlic, mix well and cook for 3 minutes to soften the onions a little.

3. Add half of the Lebanese 7-spice, mix well, and cook for 2 minutes. Tip the beef back into the pot, add the tomato purée and cook for 5 minutes, until the purée turns a dark red colour, but is not burnt.

4. Add your beef stock, passata, remaining 7-spice and the cloves, and bring the liquid to the boil. Cover the pot with the lid, reduce the heat and simmer for 1 hour, until the beef is almost tender.

5. Add the cannellini beans, then leave the lid off and simmer for 20 minutes, until the beef is tender and the sauce reduced. Remove from the heat, add salt to taste and stir through the chopped coriander. Mix well, then serve with vermicelli rice.

Serving suggestion
Vermicelli Rice (see page 206)

POULTRY

CHIPOTLE CHICKEN STEW	66
SUDADO DE POLLO	68
POLLO GUISADO (DOMINICAN REPUBLIC)	70
PIRI PIRI STEW	72
SECO DE GALLINA	74
FRANGO ESTUFADO	76
LEFTOVER TURKEY STEW	78
TAGINE MCHERMEL	80
OBE ATA	84
FESENJAN	86
GULAI AYUM	88
POLLO GUISADO (EL SALVADOR)	90
AJI DE GALLINA	92

MEXICO

SERVES FOUR

CHIPOTLE CHICKEN STEW

 24 HRS

This recipe means a lot to me – it was one of the first stews I learned to make as a student and was one of the early staple recipes of xavskitchen, setting the pace for the stews to come. When I got to uni, my mother gave me a set of chipotle pastes as part of a settling-in parcel, and my experiments with them led me to this. The paste is the secret: it packs such an incredible flavour.

PREP
15 MINS
plus marinating

COOK
50 MINS

4 skin-on chicken drumsticks
4 bone-in, skin-on chicken thighs
1 tbsp sunflower oil
½ onion, finely diced
2 garlic cloves, minced
1½ tsp tomato purée
2 tsp chipotle paste
110ml white wine
100g passata
350ml chicken stock
1 tsp dried oregano
½ tsp smoked paprika
½ tsp ground cumin
80g sweet potato, peeled and diced
½ small potato, peeled and diced
50g frozen peas
10g fresh coriander, leaves picked and roughly chopped
salt

MARINADE
4 tsp chipotle paste
1 tsp ground cumin
2 tsp smoked paprika
2 tbsp extra virgin olive oil
½ tsp salt

Serving suggestions
white rice, sliced avocado, lime wedges

1. In a large bowl, mix together all the ingredients for the marinade. Add the chicken pieces and stir until they are well coated. Cover the bowl and let the chicken marinate for 20 minutes, if you have time. If not, you can use it right away.

2. Heat up a large stew pot on a high heat and add the sunflower oil. Once hot, add all the chicken pieces and sear for 2 minutes on each side, until golden brown all over (do this in batches, if necessary). Remove the chicken from the pot and set aside.

3. Lower the heat to medium and add the onion and a pinch of salt to the pot. Sauté for 4 minutes, then add the garlic, tomato purée and chipotle paste and cook for 5 minutes, until the mixture is catching on parts of the bottom of the pot (this is where the flavour comes in). Deglaze the pot with the white wine and simmer until reduced by half (about 5 minutes), as you scrape off the stuck bits on the bottom of the pot.

4. Add the passata, chicken stock, oregano, paprika and cumin, bring the liquid to the boil, then add the chicken back in, and cover the pot with the lid. Cook the chicken for 20 minutes, then remove the lid and add both the potatoes. Simmer, uncovered, for 10 minutes, then add the frozen peas and simmer for another 5 minutes, until the stew is thickened and the peas are hot through. Stir in the chopped coriander just before serving with rice and avocado, and lime wedges for squeezing over.

COLOMBIA

SUDADO DE POLLO

SERVES FOUR

Colombia's answer to chicken stew comes in the form of the delightful sudado de pollo. For me, the real star of this dish is the cassava. I admit, I wasn't so much of a cassava fan until I learned properly how to use it. In a stew, it imparts a distinct, earthy flavour but is also great at absorbing all the other rich flavours of the broth and the seasonings. I ate this a lot while living in Spain, where I had access to so many unusual Latin American ingredients. A local shopkeeper suggested I try cassava and I'm so glad I did! It's a game-changer.

PREP
15 MINS
plus marinating

COOK
1 HR 5 MINS

- 4 bone-in, skin-on chicken thighs
- 4 skin-on chicken drumsticks
- ¼ tsp salt, plus extra to season
- 2 tbsp vegetable oil
- 1 red onion, finely diced
- ½ red pepper, deseeded and finely diced
- 2 garlic cloves, minced
- 2 tsp ground cumin
- 1 tsp sweet paprika
- 1 tsp garlic powder
- 1 tsp orange food colouring/achiote powder for colour (optional)
- 2 bay leaves
- 1½ tbsp tomato purée
- 1 tsp red pepper paste
- 100g passata
- 450ml chicken stock
- ½ tsp ground white pepper
- 1 small potato, peeled and quartered
- 80g cassava, peeled and cut into 2cm cubes
- 15g fresh coriander, leaves picked and chopped

Serving suggestions
white rice, fried plantain slices or Tostones (see page 213), diced avocado, lime wedges

1. Season your chicken pieces with the ¼ teaspoon of salt, then set them aside for at least 30 minutes, or preferably between 2 hours and overnight, covered, in the fridge. Bring to room temperature before cooking (30–60 minutes).

2. Heat up a large stew pot on a medium-high heat and add the oil. Once hot, add all the chicken and sear for 2 minutes on each side, until browned all over (do this in batches, if necessary). Remove the chicken from the pot and set aside on a plate. Reduce the heat to medium and add the onion and red pepper to the pot, with a pinch of salt, and sauté for 5 minutes, until soft.

3. Add the garlic and soften for 1 minute, then add the ground cumin, sweet paprika, garlic powder, orange food colouring or achiote powder (if using) and the bay leaves, and mix well. Add the tomato purée and red pepper paste, mix well and cook until the pastes turn a dark red colour, but are not burnt.

4. Add the passata and chicken stock, then season with the white pepper. Mix to make sure everything is combined. Add the chicken back to the pot, bring the liquid to a simmer, cover the pot with the lid and simmer for 15 minutes, until the chicken is almost cooked through.

5. Add the potato and cassava, then part-cover the pot with the lid and simmer for 25 minutes, until everything is cooked through. Remove the lid and simmer, uncovered, for a further 10 minutes, until the stew has reduced and you are left with a lovely, thick stew. Finish by sprinkling in the coriander. Serve with rice, fried plantain slices or tostones, diced avocado, and lime wedges for squeezing over.

DOMINICAN REPUBLIC

POLLO GUISADO

SERVES TWO

This homely stew from the Dominican Republic uses a method common in the Caribbean called 'browning': sugar is almost burnt in the stew pot to give the resulting stew its characteristic brown colour. What I love about this one, though, is that there is clear Spanish influence in here, too, with the tomato purée and oregano. It's a brilliant blend of cultures and flavours.

PREP
10 MINS
plus brining and marinating

COOK
55 MINS

½ lime, juiced
¼ tsp salt, plus extra to season
2 bone-in, skinless chicken thighs
2 skinless chicken drumsticks
½ tbsp vegetable oil
½ tbsp caster sugar
1 tbsp tomato purée
½ red pepper, deseeded and sliced
½ green pepper, deseeded and sliced
½ onion, sliced
280ml chicken stock

MARINADE
½ lime, juiced
2 tbsp Green Seasoning (optional; see page 210)
1 tsp dried oregano
1 tsp garlic powder
½ tsp salt
½ tsp ground white pepper
1½ tsp ground cumin
1 tsp sweet paprika
½ tsp chilli powder

Serving suggestions
Tostones (see page 213), white rice, sliced avocado, lime wedges

1. Three-quarters fill a large bowl with water and add the lime juice and ¼ teaspoon of salt. Add the chicken pieces and leave them to sit in the citrusy brine for 15 minutes. Meanwhile, mix all the marinade ingredients together. Once the 15 minutes are up, drain away the brine, then stir the marinade through the chicken. Let the chicken marinate for at least 20 minutes, but preferably overnight, covered, in the fridge, for maximum flavour (bring the chicken up to room temperature before you make the stew).

2. To start the stew, heat up a large pot on a medium-high heat and add the oil. Once hot, add the caster sugar and slowly stir. Stir frequently until the sugar starts to bubble and turn a dark brown but is not burnt. (Burnt sugar will cause the stew to taste bitter, so if you cook it for too long, discard it and start again.)

3. Add the chicken pieces to the pot (reserve the marinade in the bowl) and sear them for 2 minutes on each side, until brown all over (do this in batches, if necessary). Cover the pot with the lid and leave the chicken to cook for 5–10 minutes. During this time, the chicken will begin to release some of its juices and a beautiful light brown colour will start to form in the bottom of the pot.

4. After about 5–10 minutes (depending on how much liquid has been released), remove the lid. Using a wooden spoon, push all the chicken pieces to the edge of the pot in a ring, leaving a space in the middle. Add the tomato purée to the space and mix well in the centre of the pot until lightly browned, then add the red and green peppers and the onion, and mix for 2 minutes.

5. Pour the chicken stock into the bowl with the marinade juices and swirl to combine. Add this mixture to the stew pot and mix well. Bring the stew to a light simmer, then cover the pot with the lid and simmer for 20 minutes.

6. Remove the lid, taste, and adjust the salt levels to your preference, then leave the stew to simmer, uncovered, for a further 15 minutes, until the chicken is tender. Serve.

MOZAMBIQUE

PIRI PIRI STEW

SERVES FOUR

This is a bold and fiery stew from the African country of Mozambique, combining spicy piri piri chilli with tangy lemon to create a colourful circus of flavour. In Portugal, I lived next to the best piri piri spot in Porto, and I practically bathed their famous Frango Assado (roast chicken) in piri piri sauce. Being also a stew-lover, I decided to turn this into a stew. I played around with the flavours and spices, then finally came up with my recipe. Let me tell you, the key is the fresh mint. It really balances everything out to give you an absolutely wonderful bowl of stew!

PREP 10 MINS

COOK 45 MINS

1 tbsp vegetable oil
4 bone-in, skin-on chicken thighs
4 skin-on chicken drumsticks
1 red onion, finely diced
½ red pepper, deseeded and finely diced
5 garlic cloves, minced
2 tsp piri piri seasoning
1 tsp smoked paprika
1½ tbsp red pepper paste
2 tbsp tomato purée
750ml chicken stock
2 tsp dried oregano
1 tsp finely grated lemon zest
300g passata
20g flat-leaf parsley, leaves and stems finely chopped, plus extra leaves to serve
8 mint leaves, finely chopped, plus extra to serve
piri piri sauce, to taste
salt and black pepper

Serving suggestions
white rice, peri-salted chips

1. Heat a large stew pot on a medium-high heat, then add the vegetable oil. Once hot, add the chicken pieces and sear them for 2 minutes on each side, until brown all over (do this in batches, if necessary), then remove them from the pot and set aside on a plate.

2. Reduce the heat to medium. Add the onion and red pepper with a pinch of salt to the pot, and fry for 5 minutes, until soft. Add the garlic, soften for a minute, then add the piri piri seasoning and smoked paprika and cook for a further 1 minute.

3. Add the red pepper paste and tomato purée, then cook for 2 minutes, until the paste and purée turn a dark red colour, but are not burnt. Add the chicken stock, oregano, lemon zest, passata, parsley, mint and piri piri sauce to taste, then season with salt and pepper.

4. Add the chicken back to the pot. Bring the liquid to the boil, cover the pot with the lid, reduce the heat and simmer for 20 minutes. Remove the lid and leave the stew to cook for a final 15 minutes, until the chicken is cooked through and the sauce is thickened. Serve with rice or peri-salted chips, scattered with the extra parsley and mint.

ECUADOR

SECO DE GALLINA

SERVES FOUR

The Spanish word seco means 'dry', but this stew couldn't be less dry if it tried. This is a slow-cooked stew, with a rich, tangy sauce. In Ecuador, it is typically served on special occasions or at family gatherings. The clincher ingredient is beer. I've come to realise that I prefer cooking with beer than drinking it. Once reduced, the lager in this recipe provides the sauce with depth and malty sweetness, and the bitter edge is great for balancing out the really meaty flavours. Beer also tenderises the meat, making it extra-succulent.

PREP 10 MINS

COOK 1 HR 5 MINS

- 1 tbsp sunflower oil
- 4 bone-in, skin-on chicken thighs
- 4 skin-on chicken drumsticks
- 1 red onion, finely diced
- ½ red pepper, deseeded and finely diced
- ½ green pepper, deseeded and finely diced
- 1 tomato, finely diced
- 2 garlic cloves, minced
- 1 tsp achiote powder (optional, for the authentic colour)
- 2 tsp ground cumin
- 1 tsp ground coriander
- 1 tsp dried oregano
- 250ml lager
- 750ml chicken stock
- 140ml orange juice
- 20g fresh coriander, leaves and stems finely chopped
- 20g flat-leaf parsley, leaves and stems finely chopped
- salt and black pepper

Serving suggestions
white or tomato rice

1. Heat up a large stew pot on a medium-high heat and add the sunflower oil. Once hot, add the chicken pieces and sear them for 2 minutes on each side, until brown all over (do this in batches, if necessary). Remove them from the pot and set aside.

2. Lower the heat to medium, then add the onion and both peppers to the pot and sauté for 5 minutes, until soft. Add the tomato and cook for 5 minutes, until soft and broken down. Then, add the garlic, achiote powder (if using), cumin, ground coriander and oregano. Mix very well.

3. Add the lager to the pot, bring the liquid to a simmer and leave it to reduce by half (about 10 minutes). Then, add the chicken stock, orange juice, coriander and parsley and mix well. Bring the liquid to the boil, season with salt and pepper to taste, then add the chicken back to the pot.

4. Put the lid on the pot and leave to simmer for 25 minutes, then remove the lid and cook for a further 15 minutes, until the chicken is cooked through and the sauce is thickened. Serve with tomato or white rice.

PORTUGAL

FRANGO ESTUFADO

SERVES FOUR

This home-spun Portuguese stew is so simple – it involves only a handful of store-cupboard ingredients. It's up there in my list of favourite stews because of the nutmeg and wine, which provide, in turn, a sweet and nutty flavour and a complementary acidity.

PREP
10 MINS

COOK
50 MINS

8 bone-in, skin-on chicken thighs, halved
1 onion, diced
1 small carrot, peeled and diced
3 garlic cloves, minced
2 tbsp tomato purée
½ tbsp red pepper paste
150ml white wine
100g passata
400ml boiling water
½ tsp ground nutmeg
salt and pepper
chopped flat-leaf parsley, to garnish

1. Heat up a large stew pot on a medium-high heat. Meanwhile, season your chicken thighs with a generous amount of salt and pepper. Add the chicken to the pot and sear it for 2 minutes on each side, until brown all over (do this in batches, if necessary). Then remove the chicken from the pot and set aside.

2. Reduce the heat to medium. Add the onion and carrot to the pot and sauté for 5 minutes, until soft. Add the garlic and soften for 1 minute, then add the tomato purée and red pepper paste. Cook for 5 minutes, until the purée and paste turn a dark red colour, but are not burnt.

3. Add the wine to deglaze the pot, then let it simmer until reduced by half (about 10 minutes). Add the passata, boiling water and nutmeg, and season with salt to taste. Bring the liquid to a simmer, then return the chicken to the pot and put on the lid.

4. Simmer the stew for 10 minutes, then remove the lid and leave the stew to cook, uncovered, for 15 minutes, until the chicken is cooked through and the sauce has thickened nicely. Garnish with parsley and serve with white rice or rustic bread.

Serving suggestions
white rice or rustic bread

UK-INSPIRED

LEFTOVER TURKEY STEW

SERVES
TWO

My least favourite part of a roast turkey is the breast, as it can sometimes be drier or less flavoursome than the darker meat – but this stew transforms any leftovers, even the breast, into something delicious that I absolutely love to eat. So, in my view, this is the best way to use up leftovers after a Christmas or Thanksgiving feast. It certainly beats the traditional turkey sandwich.

PREP
10 MINS

COOK
55 MINS

1 tbsp olive oil
1 onion, sliced
4 large chestnut mushrooms, thinly sliced
1 tsp dried sage
4 garlic cloves, minced
250ml white wine
450ml vegetable stock
1 large rosemary sprig
6 thyme sprigs
400g cooked turkey breast, shredded
1 potato, peeled and diced
1 carrot, peeled and diced
50ml double cream
salt and black pepper

1. Heat up a large stew pot on a medium heat and add the olive oil. Once hot, add the onion and sauté for 5 minutes, until soft. Add the mushrooms and cook for 2 minutes so that they release their water. Add the sage and continue cooking until the mushrooms are very soft (about 5 minutes).

2. Add the garlic and soften for 2 minutes, then add the white wine to deglaze the pot and leave it to bubble until reduced by half (about 10 minutes).

3. Pour in the stock and add the rosemary and thyme sprigs. Bring the liquid to the boil, cover the pot with the lid, then reduce the heat and simmer for 10 minutes, until the sauce starts coming together. Add the shredded turkey, along with the potato and carrot, then cover again and simmer for a further 15 minutes, until the veg are tender.

4. Stir in the cream and cook for 5 minutes to heat it all through again. Season to taste with salt and pepper, then serve with rice and enjoy.

Serving suggestion
white rice

MOROCCO

TAGINE MCHERMEL

SERVES
FOUR

I first had this stew in a riad in Fes. The chicken fell off the bone and the sauce was to die for. It was my first introduction to preserved lemons, which showed me just how good a burst of citrus goodness can be in a stew. Serve this one with some rustic bread for mopping up the juicy, aromatic sauce or some crispy French fries.

PREP
15 MINS
plus marinating

COOK
55 MINS

- 4 skin-on chicken leg quarters
- 1 tbsp extra virgin olive oil
- 1 onion, grated
- 4 tsp garlic paste
- 3 tsp ginger paste
- ½ preserved lemon, pulp and skin separated and reserved, skin quartered
- 1 tsp Ras el Hanout (see page 209)
- ½ tsp ground cumin
- ½ tsp ground cardamom
- ½ tsp ground turmeric
- 1 tsp ground coriander
- 2 tbsp juice from the preserved lemon jar
- 3 tsp Saffron Water (see page 211)
- 8 green olives, pitted and chopped

1. Combine all the ingredients for the chicken marinade in a large bowl. Add the chicken pieces and turn to ensure the chicken is well coated. Leave for at least 1 hour, but preferably overnight, covered, in the fridge, to marinate. Bring to room temperature before cooking (30–60 minutes).

2. Heat up a large stew pot or hob-safe tagine on a medium heat and add the olive oil. Once hot, add the onion, garlic and ginger pastes and preserved lemon pulp and sauté, uncovered, for 5 minutes, until the onion is soft. Add the ras el hanout, cumin, cardamom, turmeric and coriander, and cook for 3 minutes to cook out the spices.

3. Add the marinated chicken and mix well (keep the marinade left in the bowl). Add the preserved lemon skin and juice and the saffron water, mix again, then cover the pot or tagine with the lid and leave to cook for 10 minutes, until the chicken has released its juices.

Pictured on page 82

MARINADE
5g fresh coriander, leaves and stems chopped
5g flat-leaf parsley, leaves and stems chopped
¼ preserved lemon, pulp only
2 tsp juice from the preserved lemon jar
½ tsp garlic paste
1½ tsp Ras el Hanout (see page 209)
3 tsp Saffron Water (see page 211)
½ tsp cayenne pepper
¼ tsp ground ginger
¼ tsp ground cardamom
¼ tsp ground turmeric
2 tbsp olive oil

4. Meanwhile, only if you're using a stew pot, pour 80ml of water into the marinade bowl and give it a good swill to ensure you get all the marinade off the sides. Set aside. (You don't need to swill if you're using a tagine.)

5. When the 10 minutes for the chicken are up, pour the leftover marinade from the bowl into the pot or tagine. Bring the liquid to a simmer, cover the pot or tagine with the lid, reduce the heat to low and steam everything for 25 minutes, until the chicken is cooked through.

6. Remove the lid and add the olives. Leave the tagine to cook, uncovered, for another 10 minutes, then serve with fries or bread.

Serving suggestions
French fries or bread

SERVES FOUR

NIGERIA

OBE ATA

The only way to describe this Nigerian stew is bold and fiery. The secret to getting it right is to almost burn the vegetables so that you get an amazing, smoky flavour that stews down with all the wonderful spices. I prefer to serve this with some white rice (rather than the more traditiona jollof rice) as a better complement for the boldness of the dish.

PREP
20 MINS

COOK
1 HR 10 MINS

200ml sunflower oil
16 fresh or dried curry leaves
8 bay leaves
2 tsp curry powder (spice level of your choice)
1 tsp ground turmeric
1 tsp ground white pepper
½ tsp red chilli powder
½ tsp cayenne pepper

PEPPER PASTE
2 Romano red peppers, deseeded and roughly diced
4 small, sweet orange peppers, deseeded and roughly diced
1 red pepper, deseeded and roughly diced
2 Roma tomatoes, roughly diced
1 habanero pepper, deseeded and roughly diced (optional; omit if you don't like spice, or add more if you do!)
12 garlic cloves, roughly chopped
2 red onions, roughly chopped
2 tbsp sunflower oil
salt and black pepper

STOCK
1 raw chicken (about 800g–1kg), cut into pieces
2 tsp ground ginger
4 tsp dried thyme
2 tsp onion powder
2 tsp garlic powder
2 tsp salt
2 tsp ground white pepper
2 chicken stock cubes (optional)

Serving suggestions
white rice, fried plantain slices, diced avocado

1. Make the pepper paste. Preheat your oven to 220°C/200°C fan. Put all your roughly diced and chopped veg into a roasting tin, sprinkle over the sunflower oil, season with salt and pepper, and roast it all for 20 minutes, or until the veg are lightly roasted and charred.

2. In the meantime, make the stock. In a large stockpot, bring 1.5 litres of water to the boil on a high heat and add the chicken pieces – as the water boils, scum will rise to the surface. Keep scooping it off and discarding it. Once there is no more, add all the remaining stock ingredients, cover the pot with the lid, reduce the heat and simmer for 15 minutes. Remove the chicken from the stock and pat it completely dry with kitchen paper. Reserve the chicken and the stock.

3. Heat up the 200ml of sunflower oil in a separate large pot (make sure the oil comes no more than half way up the inside of the pot) on a medium-high heat. Once hot, add the chicken pieces and fry them for 3–4 minutes, turning until golden brown all over. Remove the chicken from the pot and leave it to drain on kitchen paper. Reserve the oil in the pot. Strain the stock left in the chicken stock pot and measure out 600ml (any leftover will keep in a sealed jar in the fridge for up to 4 days). Set aside.

4. When the roasted vegetables are ready, tip them into a blender and blitz to a smooth paste.

5. Heat up another large stew pot on a medium heat and spoon 50ml of the oil you used for frying the chicken into it (discard the rest of the oil, or reuse it). Add the pepper paste, the curry leaves, bay leaves and your measured 600ml of stock. Add the curry powder, turmeric, white pepper, chilli powder and cayenne pepper and season with salt to taste. Cover the pot with the lid and simmer the mixture for 25 minutes, until it's all incorporated.

6. Add the fried chicken into the pot and mix well. Cover the pot with the lid and simmer on a medium-low heat for 20 minutes, until the chicken is fall-off-the-bone tender and the stock is full of flavour. Scoop out and discard the chicken bones before serving the stew with rice, fried plantain slices and diced avocado.

IRAN

FESENJAN

SERVES FOUR

This Persian stew is arguably the most unique recipe in the whole book – tender chicken simmered in a delicate walnut and pomegranate sauce infused with saffron and turmeric. I'm also suggesting an option where you swap out the chicken for oyster mushrooms if you want a veggie version. Trust me, whichever you choose – it's a party inside your mouth!

PREP
15 MINS

COOK
3 HRS 35 MINS

1kg bone-in, skin-on chicken pieces; or 8 king oyster mushrooms, halved
250g whole (shelled) walnuts
4 tbsp rapeseed oil
2 onions, finely diced
2 tsp ground turmeric
4 tbsp Saffron Water (see page 211)
3 tbsp pomegranate molasses
600ml vegetable stock
salt and black pepper
pomegranate seeds, to garnish

1. Generously season your chicken quarters or mushroom halves with salt and pepper, then place them in the fridge until you're ready to cook them.

2. Heat up a large skillet on a medium heat, then add your walnuts and toast them for 2–3 minutes, until fragrant – but do not burn them. Allow to cool for a few minutes, then place them in a food processor and blend until you have an ultra-smooth paste. Set the paste aside.

3. Heat up a large stew pot on a medium heat, then add the rapeseed oil. Once hot, add the onions and sauté for 5 minutes, until soft. Season with a pinch of salt and the ground turmeric, then mix well and cook for 2 minutes to cook out the spice.

4. Add the blended walnut mixture and cook for about 10 minutes, stirring frequently, until you see some bubbles appearing, which is the fat from the walnuts being released. This is the sign to add the saffron water and pomegranate molasses. Mix well.

5. Add the vegetable stock, bring the liquid to a light simmer, then reduce the heat, cover the pot with the lid and cook for 2 hours 30 minutes, until the sauce is dark brown.

6. Meanwhile, heat a large frying pan on a medium-high heat. Add your chicken or mushrooms and sear for 2 minutes on each side, until well browned all over (do this in batches, if necessary). Remove from the pan and set aside until the stew pot is ready.

7. After 2 hours 30 minutes, add the chicken or mushrooms to the stew and cook, covered, for 45 minutes, until the stew is a dark brown colour and the chicken is super-tender or the mushrooms are cooked through. Scatter with pomegranate seeds and serve with the Persian tahdig.

Serving suggestion
Persian Tahdig (see page 203)

INDONESIA

GULAI AYUM

SERVES
TWO

Travelling in Indonesia exposed me to an unbelievable number of incredible sauces, stews and soups – but I had one miss… this one, which I didn't discover until I started looking into the specifics of Indonesian cooking when I got home. As soon as I found it, I knew that it was a bit of me, so I began to develop this recipe and make it my own. It's tender cuts of chicken simmered down in a spiced, coconut-based sauce infused with lemongrass, tamarind, star anise and lime leaves, and stewed until that chicken is falling off the bone.

PREP
15 MINS

plus marinating

COOK
1 HR 15 MINS

2 skin-on chicken drumsticks
2 bone-in, skin-on chicken thighs
2 tbsp peanut oil
150ml coconut milk
1 lemongrass stalk, bashed
2 makrut lime leaves
1½ tsp sweet soy sauce
1 star anise
2 tsp tamarind paste
350ml chicken stock
salt and black pepper

SPICE PASTE
15g fresh ginger, peeled
2 spring onions, green parts only
20g fresh galangal, peeled
6 garlic cloves, peeled
½ tsp red chilli powder
½ tsp ground cardamom
¼ tsp ground cumin
½ tsp ground cinnamon
¼ tsp ground nutmeg
¼ tsp ground turmeric
1 tsp smoked paprika
1 tsp ground black pepper
1 tsp salt
2 tbsp sunflower oil

Serving suggestion
white rice

1. Season all your chicken with a generous amount of salt and pepper, then leave to marinate for 30 minutes in the fridge (bring up to room temperature before cooking). Meanwhile, make the spice paste. Put all the ingredients and 2 tablespoons of water into a blender and blitz to a paste. Set aside.

2. When the chicken is ready, heat up a large stew pot on a medium-high heat, then add the peanut oil. Once hot, add the chicken pieces and sear them for 2 minutes on each side, until golden all over (do this in batches, if necessary). Remove the meat from the pot and set aside. Add the spice paste to the pot and cook it for 5 minutes, until it's reduced down.

3. Pour in the coconut milk, then add the lemongrass, lime leaves, sweet soy sauce, star anise, tamarind paste and chicken stock. Season to taste with salt, then bring the liquid to the boil. Reduce the heat, put the lid on the pot and simmer the mixture for 30 minutes. Then, add the chicken back to the pot and part-cover it with the lid. Simmer for 25 minutes, until the chicken is cooked through.

4. Remove the lid from the pot and leave the stew to cook for a further 10 minutes, to thicken. Serve with rice.

EL SALVADOR

SERVES TWO

POLLO GUISADO

This stew from El Salvador uses arguably one of the most interesting cooking methods I have witnessed. The dish starts off with a 'relax', a spice mix of annatto, sesame seeds, peanuts, cayenne, guajillo chilli and more. This is added to a stew pot, then cooked with chicken marinated in mustard, with carrot and potato. The resulting stew is fragrant and vibrant. It's a flavour profile that – so far – feels unique to me; a fusion of West African, South American and Mexican cooking. Amazing.

PREP
15 MINS

COOK
1 HR 5 MINS

2 skin-on chicken drumsticks
2 bone-in, skin-on chicken thighs
1 tsp olive oil
200ml chicken stock
½ small carrot, peeled and cut into 2cm cubes
½ small potato, peeled and cut into 2cm cubes

MARINADE
½ tsp salt
1 tsp Dijon mustard
1 tbsp Worcestershire sauce
1 tsp all-purpose seasoning (I use the Hispanic brand Goya, for authenticity)

'RELAX'
1 tsp annatto seeds
4 tbsp unsalted peanuts
1 guajillo chilli
1 tsp sesame seeds
1 tbsp olive oil
1 tomato, diced
3 garlic cloves, minced
½ onion, diced
½ tsp dried thyme
¼ tsp cayenne pepper
1 tsp Sazón Goya (with annatto)

1. Put all the marinade ingredients in a large bowl and stir to combine. Add the chicken pieces and turn them to coat fully. Set aside until you're ready to use them.

2. To make the 'relax', heat up a large skillet or frying pan on a medium heat. Add the annatto seeds, peanuts, guajillo chilli and sesame seeds and toast them until fragrant but not burnt (about 30–40 seconds). Remove them from the pan to a plate and set aside.

3. In the same pan, heat the olive oil and add the tomato, garlic and onion and sauté for about 5 minutes, until the onion is soft. Tip this, as well as the toasted seeds mixture and all the remaining 'relax' ingredients into a food processor and blend until smooth (add a little cold water if it's too thick). Set aside.

4. For the stew, heat up a large stew pot on a medium-high heat and add the teaspoon of olive oil. Once hot, add the marinated chicken and sear for 2 minutes on each side, until browned all over. Remove the chicken from the pot and set it aside. Pour the prepared 'relax' and the chicken stock into the pot, then bring the liquid to a light simmer. Cover with the lid, reduce the heat and simmer for 20 minutes, until fragrant.

5. Add the chicken, carrot and potato to the pot, cover with the lid again and simmer for 20 minutes, until the chicken is cooked through and the vegetables are nearly tender.

6. Remove the lid and cook for a further 15 minutes, until the stew has reduced. Serve with rice, sliced avocado and lime wedges for squeezing over.

PERU

AJI DE GALLINA

SERVES TWO

This is Peru's answer to comfort food – a fiery chicken stew with a red onion, garlic and chilli-based sofrito, infused with oregano, cumin and coriander. Aji amarillo, a mildly hot, orange-coloured chilli from South America, is my new obsession. It is slightly sweet with a subtle, berry-like flavour. The paste is perfect in this stew, but also on eggs. I add it to omelettes and scrambled eggs, and I even dot it over boiled eggs. It has a really distinct and special flavour.

PREP
20 MINS

COOK
1 HR 15 MINS

STOCK
½ carrot, peeled and chopped
1 celery stick, including leaves
½ red onion, chopped
4 garlic cloves, peeled but left whole
10g fresh coriander, leaves and stems
1 bay leaf
1 tsp cumin seeds
½ tsp dried oregano
1 tsp salt, plus extra to season
2 large boneless, skinless chicken breasts (350–400g in total)

BREAD PASTE
50g plain white bread
2 tbsp evaporated milk
1 tbsp whole milk
100ml chicken stock (see above)

STEW
1 tbsp vegetable oil
½ red onion, finely diced
½ tsp ground cumin
1 tsp dried oregano
1 tsp garlic paste
4 tsp aji amarillo paste
10g pecan nuts, finely chopped, plus extra halves to serve
20g Parmesan cheese, grated
2 tbsp evaporated milk
salt and black pepper

Serving suggestions
white rice, black olives, soft-boiled egg (peeled and halved)

1. Make the chicken stock. Bring 1 litre of water to the boil in a large pot. Add the carrot, celery, onion, garlic, coriander, bay leaf, cumin seeds, oregano and the measured salt, then cover the pot with the lid. Lower the heat and simmer for 15 minutes, to infuse the flavours. Add the chicken breasts, replace the lid and simmer for 25 minutes, until the chicken is cooked through. Remove from the heat and scoop out the breasts. Shred the meat and set it aside for later. Measure out 300ml of the stock and set that aside for the bread paste and stew (save the remainder for another time – it will keep in an airtight jar in the fridge for up to 4 days).

2. Make the bread paste by combining all the bread paste ingredients in a blender or food processor and blitzing until smooth. Set aside.

3. For the stew, heat up a large stew pot on a medium heat, then add the vegetable oil. Once hot, add the onion and sauté for 5 minutes, until soft. Add the cumin and oregano, mix well and cook for 2 minutes to cook out the spice. Add the garlic paste and aji amarillo paste and fry on a medium-low heat for 5 minutes, until thick.

4. Add the bread paste, then mix well. Little by little, pour in the remaining 200ml of chicken stock, stirring after each addition until smooth, then once all the stock is in, add the pecan nuts and cook for 15 minutes, until well incorporated and thick.

5. Using a hand-held stick blender, blend the stew sauce until it is nice and smooth. Return the pot to a medium heat, add the shredded chicken, the Parmesan and evaporated milk and mix well. Leave to simmer for 5 minutes to heat through. Season with salt and pepper to taste. Serve with white rice, black olives and soft-boiled egg halves, and sprinkled with the extra pecans.

BEEF

CHILLI CON CARNE	96
BEEF BOURGUIGNON	98
MISO SHORT RIB	100
JARDINEIRA	102
FLEMISH STEW	104
POTJIEKOS	106
RABO DE TORO	110
KERALA BEEF STEW	112
CODA ALLA VACINNARA	114
STIFADO	116
BO KHO	118
RENDANG	120
OXTAIL KIMCHI STEW	122
CHILE COLORADO	124

USA

CHILLI CON CARNE

SERVES FOUR

With its roots in Tex-Mex cuisine, this is a comforting combination of beef and beans that is simmered down in a rich, spicy, tomato-based sauce. This version is one I've developed over the years – I started making it as a basic student staple, with limited ingredients. Then, as I fell in love with cooking, my spice cupboard took on a life of its own and before long I seemed to have every spice going. I began to experiment with different rubs until I found my formula. And then I added dark cocoa powder – my (until now) secret ingredient.

PREP
15 MINS

COOK
45 MINS

2 tbsp sunflower oil
1 red onion, finely diced
½ red pepper, deseeded and finely diced
½ green pepper, deseeded and finely diced
4 garlic cloves, minced
500g beef mince (20% fat)
6 tsp tomato purée
3 tsp chipotle paste
200ml red wine
1 x 400g can red kidney beans, drained and rinsed
160g passata
150ml beef stock
½ tsp dark cocoa powder
20g fresh coriander, leaves picked and chopped
1 lime, juiced
salt and black pepper

SPICE MIX
1 tsp ground cinnamon
½ tsp ground cayenne pepper
1½ tsp sweet paprika
2 tsp smoked paprika
a pinch of ground nutmeg
1 tsp chilli powder
2 tsp dried oregano
1 tsp ground cumin

Serving suggestions
white rice, sour cream, lime wedges, chopped avocado

1. Combine all the spices and the oregano for the spice mix in a small bowl and set aside.

2. Heat up a large stew pot on a medium heat and add the oil. Once hot, add the onion and both peppers and cook for 5 minutes, until soft. Add the garlic and soften for 1 minute. Add the beef mince and sear for 5 minutes, until brown all over.

3. Add the tomato purée and chipotle paste and cook for 5 minutes, until darkened but not burnt. Deglaze the pot with the red wine and leave it to bubble away, until the liquid has reduced by half (about 10 minutes). Once reduced, add the beans and passata and mix very well. Pour in the beef stock along with the spice mix and the cocoa powder. Mix well, then bring the liquid to the boil. Cover the pot with a lid, reduce the heat and simmer for at least 20 minutes or up to 2 hours – the longer the better – until everything is cooked through.

4. Remove the lid and leave the chilli to simmer, uncovered, for 10 minutes. Taste and season with salt and pepper. Add the coriander and mix well, then remove the pot from the heat and finish off with the lime juice.

FRANCE

BEEF BOURGUIGNON

SERVES FOUR

This is a French classic: tender beef shins stewed down in a rich, red wine sauce, infused with fresh herbs and finished off with sweet pearly onions. This was the stew that helped put xavskitchen on the map. I uploaded it on a random Tuesday in May 2023 and before I knew it, it had gone viral with over 15 million views, bringing in hundreds of thousands of followers. I used this momentum to fuel my Stews from Around the World series. Apart from the social-media success it's brought, this stew is a genuine delight to eat.

PREP 15 MINS

COOK 3 HRS

1 tsp sunflower oil
500g beef shin, cut into 5cm cubes
140g smoked back bacon, chopped
1 onion, finely diced
4 garlic cloves, minced
80g chestnut mushrooms, quartered
300ml good-quality red wine
550ml beef stock
10 thyme sprigs or 1 tbsp dried thyme
1 rosemary sprig or 1 tbsp dried rosemary
2 bay leaves
½ tsp ground black pepper
1½ tsp cocoa powder
1 small carrot, sliced
15 small silverskin (pearl) onions
20g flat-leaf parsley, leaves picked and finely chopped, plus extra to garnish
1 tbsp plain flour, if needed

Serving suggestions
boiled new potatoes or mashed potatoes, salad

1. Heat up a large stew pot on a medium heat and add the sunflower oil. Once hot, add the beef and sear for 5 minutes, turning, until well browned all over (do this in batches, if necessary). Remove the beef from the pot and set aside. Add the bacon to the pot, increase the heat to medium-high and cook for 1 minute, until some of the fat has rendered. Then, add the onion, reduce the heat to medium and sauté for 5 minutes, until the onion is soft.

2. Add the garlic, soften for 1 minute, then add the mushrooms and sauté for 5 minutes to colour. Return the beef to the pot, pour in the red wine and let it simmer for about 10 minutes, until it has reduced by half.

3. Add the beef stock, thyme, rosemary, bay leaves, black pepper and cocoa powder, then bring everything to a simmer. Put the lid on the pot and simmer gently for 1 hour 45 minutes, until the beef is tender.

4. Add the carrot to the pot and leave the stew to cook uncovered for 30 minutes to thicken the gravy.

5. Add the silverskin onions and parsley and heat through for 10 minutes. The stew should be nice and thick at this point so you shouldn't need any flour, but if it isn't, remove the pot from the heat, sift in the tablespoon of flour and whisk it into the stew. Allow the flour to cook out for about 10–15 minutes, until the stew is thickened. Serve garnished with the extra parsley, with a salad and boiled new potatoes or mashed potatoes on the side.

JAPAN

MISO SHORT RIB

SERVES
FOUR

This one is a real crowd-pleaser – it's always love at first bite. You get the rich notes from the beef ribs, balanced so well with the salty miso and the acidity from the makrut lime leaves to form a wonderfully harmonious blend of flavours that I adore!

PREP
10 MINS

COOK
2 HRS 20 MINS

1 tbsp vegetable oil
1kg beef short ribs
2 onions, finely diced
80g leek, finely diced
15g fresh ginger, peeled and minced
8 garlic cloves, minced
6 tsp brown miso paste
4 makrut lime leaves
6 tsp mirin
2 tsp fish sauce
4 tsp sweet soy sauce
750ml beef stock

1. Heat a large stew pot on a medium-high heat. Add the vegetable oil, then once hot, add the beef ribs and sear them for 5 minutes, turning, until well browned all over (do this in batches, if necessary). Remove the ribs from the pot and set aside. Add the onions and leek to the pot and sauté for 5 minutes, until soft. Add the ginger and garlic and soften for 1 minute, until soft and fragrant.

2. Add the miso paste, mix well, reduce the heat to medium and cook for 5 minutes, until darkened. Add the short ribs back to the pot, then add all the remaining ingredients. Mix well and bring to the boil, then reduce the heat, put a lid on the pot and simmer for 2 hours, until tender. Alternatively at this point, you can braise the stew in a preheated oven at 190°C/170°C fan for 2 hours 30 minutes. Serve with bread or mashed potatoes.

Serving suggestions
bread or mashed potatoes

PORTUGAL

JARDINEIRA

SERVES
FOUR

Named using the Portuguese word for 'gardener', the jardineira is a rich meat stew and a backbone of loads of vegetables – peas, beans, carrots and potatoes in this case, but any seasonal veg would do. When I lived in Portugal, this was a real end-of-the-week treat made with authentic Portuguese chouriço, which I bought from a lady who promised me she was selling the best chouriço to make a jardineira.

PREP
15 MINS

COOK
2 HRS 30 MINS

2 tbsp sunflower oil
1kg beef shin, cut into 5cm cubes
280g Portuguese chouriço (or regular chorizo), cut into 1cm slices
160g smoked back bacon, diced
2 onions, diced
8 garlic cloves, minced
350ml white wine
200g passata
750ml beef stock
4 tsp sweet paprika
2 tsp smoked paprika
2 small carrots, peeled and chopped into 2cm chunks
2 small potatoes, peeled and chopped into 2cm chunks
4 flat or runner beans, cut into 3cm chunks
120g frozen peas
salt and black pepper
chopped flat-leaf parsley, to garnish

1. Put a large stew pot on a medium heat and add the sunflower oil. Once hot, add the beef and sear it for 5 minutes, turning, until browned all over (do this in batches, if necessary), then remove from the pot and set aside. Add the chouriço and bacon, then cook for 2 minutes to brown slightly and render some of the fat. Add the onions and garlic and cook for 4 minutes more, until fragrant and soft.

2. Add the beef back to the pot, then pour in the white wine and simmer for 10 minutes, until reduced by half. Add the passata, beef stock and sweet and smoked paprikas. Bring the pot to a simmer, then reduce the heat, cover with the lid and cook for 1 hour 30 minutes, until the beef is almost tender.

3. Taste the stew and season with salt to your preference, then add the carrots and potatoes and cook, uncovered, for a further 20 minutes, until the vegetables are tender.

4. Add the runner beans, cook for 10 minutes, then finally add the peas and cook for a further 5 minutes, until the beans and peas are cooked through. Season to taste with salt and pepper, garnish with parsley, then serve with bread.

Serving suggestion
bread

BELGIUM

FLEMISH STEW

SERVES
FOUR

The beauty of this Belgian stew lies in the beer – dark ale is best. Once reduced, the ale provides the broth with a uniquely rich, slightly bitter and sweet flavour, which is – honestly – finger-licking. Serve this one up with Belgian fries.

PREP
10 MINS

COOK
2 HRS 30 MINS

2 tbsp unsalted butter
½ tbsp sunflower oil
500g beef shin, cut into 5cm cubes
1 onion, finely chopped
1 tsp ground black pepper
4 garlic cloves, minced
450ml dark ale
425ml beef stock
2 tbsp syrup de liege (or use pear jam)
5 thyme sprigs or 1 tbsp dried thyme
1 slice of rye bread
2 tsp Dijon mustard
salt

1. Heat up a large stew pot on a medium-high heat. Once hot, add the butter and sunflower oil. Add the beef and sear it for 5 minutes, turning, until browned all over (do this in batches, if necessary). Remove the beef from the pot and set aside.

2. Add the onion to the pot with a pinch of salt and the black pepper, then cook on a medium heat for 5 minutes, until soft. Add the garlic and soften for 1 minute. Return the beef to the pot, then pour in the dark ale. It's crucial to cook out the alcohol from the ale properly – leave it to bubble away, uncovered, for 10–15 minutes, until significantly reduced. The alcohol must be cooked out before you cover the pot, otherwise the stew will taste bitter.

3. Add the beef stock, syrup de liege (or pear jam) and thyme and mix well. Bring the liquid to a simmer.

4. Spread the rye bread with the mustard and place this on top of the simmering stew – just leave it there and cover the pot with the lid. Simmer away on a medium heat for 20 minutes, then remove the lid, mix well, then cover again and cook for 1 hour 30 minutes on a low heat, until tender.

5. Once the beef is cooked and meltingly tender, remove the lid and leave the stew to gently simmer for a further 15 minutes, until reduced to a thick consistency. Serve with Belgian fries.

Serving suggestion
Belgian fries

SOUTH AFRICA

POTJIEKOS

SERVES TWO

Traditionally cooked in a three-legged pot known as a potjie, over a fire, this hearty and aromatic oxtail stew originates from South Africa. It's unusual because the oxtail chunks are simmered in a broth, with the spices, until tender, and then fresh vegetables are layered over the top, without stirring, until cooked through. Even if you don't have a potjie, the combination of spices and rich, tender meat and veg make this stew amazing.

PREP 15 MINS

COOK 3 HRS

1 tbsp sunflower oil
400g oxtail chunks, trimmed
½ tsp yellow mustard seeds
1 tsp cumin seeds
½ onion, diced
½ tsp ground ginger
1 tsp garam masala
1 tsp ground cumin
½ tsp cayenne pepper
1 tsp dried mixed herbs
250ml red wine
450ml beef stock
2 bay leaves
8 thyme sprigs
1 small carrot, peeled and quartered
150g sweet potato, peeled and quartered
350g peeled and deseeded butternut squash, quartered
2 corn-on-the-cobs, each chopped into thick slices
6 white mushrooms, thinly sliced
2 cabbage leaves, quartered
salt

1. Put a large stew pot on a medium-high heat and add the sunflower oil. Once hot, add the oxtail pieces and sear, turning, for 5 minutes, until brown all over (do this in batches, if necessary). Remove the meat from the pot and set aside. In the same pot, add the mustard and cumin seeds and fry for 30 seconds. Add the onion and a pinch of salt and fry for 5 minutes, until soft.

2. Reduce the heat to medium, then add all the spices and the mixed herbs and cook for 2 minutes. Add the oxtail back to the pot and pour in the red wine to deglaze. Simmer until reduced by half (about 10 minutes), then add the beef stock, bay leaves and thyme sprigs. Bring the liquid to a simmer, then cover the pot with the lid and cook for 2 hours, until the oxtail is almost tender.

3. The traditional way of making the potjiekos is to layer the vegetables without stirring. So, add the carrot and sweet potato in layers on top of the stew and cook for 10 minutes. Then, add the squash, corn pieces and mushrooms, again in layers, and cook for a further 10 minutes. Finally, add the cabbage leaves and let them steam for 10 minutes, until all the vegetable layers are tender and the oxtail is falling off the bone. Serve with bread or rice.

Serving suggestions
bread or white rice

SPAIN

RABO DE TORO

SERVES
FOUR

A university friend of mine introduced me to this iconic Spanish oxtail stew (the name literally translates as 'tail of the bull'). Tender cuts of oxtail are slow-cooked in a herby, rich, tomato, carrot, leek and red wine sauce, until they are melt-in-the-mouth tender. I like to think of it as a fiesta in every bite! Crispy fried potato wedges are the perfect accompaniment.

PREP
15 MINS

COOK
3 HRS 20 MINS

200g plain flour
1 tsp salt, plus extra to season
2 tsp ground black pepper
1kg oxtail chunks, trimmed
5 tsp olive oil, plus extra if needed
1 Spanish sweet onion, diced
1 small carrot, peeled and diced into small cubes
150g leek, diced
4 garlic cloves, minced
400ml red wine
150g passata
800ml beef stock
2 rosemary sprigs or 2 tbsp dried rosemary
8 thyme sprigs or 2 tbsp dried thyme
4 bay leaves
14g piece of 70% dark chocolate

1. Tip the flour into a large mixing bowl. Season with the measured salt and the black pepper and stir to combine. Add the oxtail pieces and turn them through the seasoned flour to coat, ensuring each piece is well covered.

2. Heat up a large stew pot on a medium-high heat and add the olive oil. Once hot, add the oxtail pieces to the pot and sear them, turning frequently to avoid burning the flour, for 2 minutes, until brown all over (do this in batches, if necessary). Remove the meat from the pot and set aside.

3. Add a dash more olive oil to the pot if needed, then add the onion, carrot and leek with a pinch of salt. Reduce the heat to medium and fry for 5 minutes, until the onion is soft. Add the garlic and soften for 1 minute.

4. Add the oxtail pieces back to the pot, then pour in the red wine. Leave the wine to bubble away until it is reduced by half (about 10 minutes). Add the passata and beef stock and bring the liquid to the boil. Add the rosemary, thyme, bay leaves and whole piece of chocolate. Reduce the heat, put the lid on the pot and simmer for 3 hours, until the oxtail is fall-off-the-bone tender.

5. Remove the tender oxtail pieces and set them aside (discard the bones, if you prefer). Using a hand-held stick blender, off the heat, blitz the rest of the stew to form a smooth sauce. Serve the sauce over the oxtail with some fried wedges or chips.

Serving suggestions
fried potato wedges or chips

INDIA

SERVES FOUR

KERALA BEEF STEW

This rich, coconut-based stew is to die for – but, then, as you may know, I'm a big fan of coconuts. I love how the stew is altogether bold and rich, but provides lovely hints of delicate spice in every mouthful. Serve it simply, with some white rice, so that the layers of flavour take centre stage. They deserve it.

PREP
15 MINS

COOK
3 HRS

1 tbsp sunflower oil
750g beef shin, cut into 4cm chunks
1 red onion, sliced
3 garlic cloves, minced
thumb-sized piece of fresh ginger, peeled and finely chopped
1 green chilli (deseed according to your preference for heat), finely chopped
1 cinnamon stick
5 cloves
½ tsp fennel seeds
3 green cardamom pods
3 tsp garam masala
200ml coconut milk
400ml beef stock
100ml coconut cream
1 large carrot, peeled and cut into 2cm cubes
1 potato, peeled and cut into 2cm cubes
1 tbsp coconut oil
2 shallots, finely sliced
2 dried red chillies
5 fresh curry leaves (or use dried, if necessary)
salt and black pepper

1. Put a large stew pot on a medium-high heat and add the sunflower oil. Once hot, add the beef and sear for 5 minutes, turning, until browned all over (do this in batches, if necessary). Remove the beef from the pot and set aside.

2. Add the onion, garlic, ginger and green chilli to the pot and cook for 1 minute, to soften. Add the cinnamon stick, cloves, fennel seeds and green cardamom pods, reduce the heat to medium and cook for 5 minutes, until fragrant.

3. Spoon in half of the garam masala and mix well. Add the beef back to the pot, along with the coconut milk and beef stock and season with salt and pepper to taste. Cover the pot with the lid, reduce the heat and simmer for 2 hours, until the beef is tender.

4. Add the coconut cream, carrot and potato, then mix well. Add the remaining garam masala, part-cover the pot with the lid and simmer for a further 30 minutes, until incorporated well into the sauce.

5. Put a frying pan on a medium-high heat and add the coconut oil. Once melted and hot, add the shallots, dried red chillies and curry leaves and fry until fragrant (about 30 seconds). Tip the contents of the frying pan into the stew pot, mix well and cook for a further 10 minutes, uncovered. Adjust the seasoning to taste and serve with white rice.

Serving suggestion
white rice

ITALY

CODA ALLA VACINNARA

SERVES FOUR

If you ever find yourself in the bustling streets of Trastevere in Rome, you may stumble across this classic Roman dish. Succulent pieces of oxtail are simmered down in an aromatic base of onion, carrot and celery, enriched with white wine and lightly infused with cloves, then finished off with cocoa powder, raisins and pine nuts. Perfection.

PREP
10 MINS

COOK
2 HRS 45 MINS

1kg oxtail chunks, trimmed
150g plain flour
1 tbsp extra virgin olive oil
2 onions, finely diced
1 celery stick, finely diced
2 carrots, peeled and finely diced
2 tbsp tomato purée
150ml white wine
300ml beef stock
200g passata
1 tsp dried thyme
½ tbsp dried rosemary
3 cloves
1 tsp cocoa powder
2 tbsp pine nuts
1 tbsp raisins
salt and black pepper

1. Season your oxtail with the flour and a pinch each of salt and pepper, ensuring each piece is well covered, then set aside.

2. Heat up a large stew pot on a medium-high heat and add the olive oil. Add the oxtail pieces to the pot and sear them for 2 minutes, turning frequently to avoid burning the flour, until browned all over (do this in batches, if necessary). Remove the meat from the pot and set aside.

3. Add your onions, celery and carrots with a pinch of salt to the pot and cook for 5 minutes, until soft. Add the oxtail back to the pot, along with the tomato purée, and cook for 3 minutes, until the purée turns a dark red colour, but is not burnt. Add the white wine and bring the liquid to a simmer. Leave it all to bubble away for about 10 minutes, until reduced by half.

4. Add the beef stock, passata, thyme, rosemary and cloves. Bring to the boil, reduce the heat, put the lid on the pot and simmer for 2 hours, or until the oxtail is falling off the bone.

5. Stir in the cocoa powder, then cook, uncovered, for 20 minutes, until the stew has reduced. Serve with the pine nuts and raisins scattered on top.

Serving suggestion
crusty bread

GREECE

STIFADO

SERVES FOUR

I love this stew so much! The ingredients give such a wide range of flavours that all come together and hit you at once. You get warming notes from the cloves, a tanginess from the white wine vinegar, and a balancing sweetness from the red wine. Then, after all of that, you get lovely fresh, earthy notes from the oregano, lemon thyme and rosemary. This had me feeling like I was back in a taverna on a beautiful Greek Island.

PREP 15 MINS

COOK 2 HRS 30 MINS

2 tbsp olive oil
900g beef shin, cut into 4cm chunks
10 small round shallots, peeled but left whole
2 onions, finely diced
½ tsp salt, plus extra to season
6 garlic cloves, minced
2 cinnamon sticks
4 bay leaves
4 cloves
2 tsp black peppercorns
8 pimento (allspice) berries
4 tsp tomato purée
400ml red wine
200g passata
600ml beef stock
2 tsp dried oregano
8 lemon thyme sprigs or 2 tsp dried lemon thyme
8 thyme sprigs or 2 tsp dried thyme
2 rosemary sprigs or 2 tsp dried rosemary
½ tsp white wine vinegar

1. Put a large stew pot on a medium-high heat and add the olive oil. Once hot, add your beef and sear, turning, for 5 minutes, until brown all over (do this in batches, if necessary). Remove the beef from the pot and set aside. Add the shallots to the pot, reduce the heat to medium and sauté for 1 minute, turning, until lightly brown all over. Remove them from the pot and set aside.

2. Add the onions with the ½ teaspoon of salt to the pot and sauté for 2 minutes, until just softening. Then, add the garlic and soften for 1 minute. Add the cinnamon sticks, bay leaves, cloves, peppercorns and pimento berries, reduce the heat to medium-low and sauté for 5 minutes, until the onions are soft and the spices are fragrant.

3. Add the purée and cook for 5 minutes, until the purée is a dark red colour, but is not burnt. Add the beef back to the pot, then add the red wine and let it reduce by half (about 10 minutes).

4. Pour in the passata and beef stock, then add the dried oregano and the lemon thyme, thyme and rosemary. Bring the liquid to the boil, then put the lid on the pot, reduce the heat to low and simmer the stew for 1 hour 40 minutes, until the beef is tender.

5. Add the white wine vinegar and return the shallots to the pot. Simmer, uncovered, for 20 minutes to heat through the shallots and thicken the stew. Serve with crusty bread.

Serving suggestion
crusty bread

VIETNAM

BO KHO

SERVES
FOUR

A Vietnamese household staple, bo kho involves slow-cooking tender beef chunks in a wonderfully fragrant coconut-based broth. This was one of the first stews I ever made. It's a really fascinating blend of flavours, and contains two of my favourite things: coconut water and lemongrass.

PREP
15 MINS
plus marinating

COOK
4 HRS 10 MINS

800g beef shin, cut into 5cm chunks
1 tbsp sunflower oil
4 shallots, finely diced
2 lemongrass stalks, bashed
2 star anise
2 cinnamon sticks
6 bay leaves
600ml coconut water
400ml beef stock
1 small carrot, peeled and sliced into 2–3cm chunks
1 potato, peeled and sliced into 2–3cm chunks

MARINADE
2 tsp coconut oil
2 tsp garlic paste
4 tsp light soy sauce
2 tsp sweet soy sauce
1 tsp fish sauce
1 tsp Chinese 5-spice
1 tsp ground ginger
½ tsp annatto powder (for colour)
1 tsp paprika
2 tsp dried thyme
1 tsp ground white pepper

1. First, combine all the ingredients for the marinade in a large bowl. Mix until you have a nice, smooth paste.

2. Add the beef to the bowl with the marinade and mix it through, ensuring that each piece is well covered. Set aside to marinate for 30 minutes in the fridge, or for the best results, a few hours. Bring to room temperature before cooking (30–60 minutes).

3. Heat up a large stew pot on a medium heat, then add the sunflower oil. Once hot, add the beef and sear it for 5 minutes, turning, until it is browned all over (do this in batches, if necessary). Remove the beef from the pot and set aside.

4. Add the shallots to the pot and cook for 2 minutes, watching closely to ensure they don't burn and are soft and lightly browned all over. Add the lemongrass stalks and leave them to release their flavour for 1 minute. Add the beef back to the pot along with the star anise, cinnamon sticks, bay leaves, coconut water and beef stock. Bring the liquid to the boil, cover the pot with the lid, reduce the heat and simmer for a minimum of 2 hours and up to 3 hours, until the beef is almost tender.

5. Remove the lid and leave the stew to simmer for 1 hour, until the beef is meltingly tender and the sauce is thick. About 25 minutes before the end of the cooking time, add the carrot and potato, so that they are cooked through by the time the beef is ready. Serve with hunks of French baguette.

Serving suggestion
French baguette

SERVES
FOUR

INDONESIA
RENDANG

A delicate balance of warming spices and bold flavours with sweet and savoury notes throughout, this is one of the most delicious and satisfying stews out there. And I have my followers to thank for it – I had so many requests for a rendang recipe that I made my way to my local Asian market in Spain, bought all the ingredients and experimented until I got it right. The result is unbelievably good.

PREP
20 MINS

COOK
3 HRS 15 MINS

1 tbsp sunflower oil
1kg beef short ribs
400ml coconut milk
100ml coconut cream
5 makrut lime leaves
1 cinnamon stick
1 star anise
1 black cardamom pod
3 lemongrass stalks, bashed
3 bay leaves
4 cloves
500ml boiling water
1 tsp palm sugar
1½ tbsp tamarind paste
salt

PASTE (REMPAH)
10 dried red chillies (I use árbol chillies)
3 shallots, chopped
6 garlic cloves, roughly chopped
10g fresh ginger, peeled
5g fresh turmeric, peeled, or 1 tsp ground turmeric
15g fresh galangal, peeled
1 lemongrass stalk, bashed and sliced

KERISIK
40g desiccated coconut

Serving suggestion
white rice

1 To make the paste, tip everything into a blender or food processor and pulse until smooth.

2 Heat up a large stew pot on a medium heat and add the oil. Once hot, add the paste and cook for 8–10 minutes, until reduced and thickened.

3 Add the beef short ribs, mix very well, cook for 5 minutes, then add the coconut milk and coconut cream and mix again. Add the lime leaves, cinnamon stick, star anise, black cardamom pod, lemongrass stalks, bay leaves, cloves and boiling water. Cover the pot with the lid, reduce the heat and simmer for 1 hour 30 minutes, until the beef is almost tender.

4 An hour into the stew cooking time, prepare your kerisik. Toast the grated coconut in a dry frying pan on a low heat until it turns a golden brown (about 8 minutes). Take care not to let the coconut burn, otherwise it will become bitter and you'll need to start again. Tip the golden coconut into a mortar and grind it with the pestle until you have a smooth brown paste.

5 Once the 1 hour 30 minutes of cooking time is up, remove the lid from the pot and add the palm sugar, tamarind paste and kerisik. Season to taste with salt, then simmer, uncovered, for another 1 hour 30 minutes, until the stew has reduced right down and is a dark brown colour. Stir frequently to avoid the stew catching as it reduces. Serve with rice.

KOREA

OXTAIL KIMCHI STEW

SERVES
FOUR

This soul-warming stew, with bags of umami, is ideal if you're after a wonderful blend of savoury and spice. It came about almost out of nowhere, after I'd been testing a bunch of other dishes. I threw together all the leftovers – lemongrass, kimchi, gochujang and oxtail – and let them simmer away for a few hours. Oh, my word. The magic! I tested it a few more times to get the quantities just right and here it is, in the book. So satisfying!

PREP
10 MINS

COOK
2 HRS 45 MINS

1kg oxtail chunks, trimmed
2 tbsp peanut oil
2 red onions, finely diced
1 tsp pimento (allspice) berries
1 tsp cumin seeds
1 tsp coriander seeds
10g fresh ginger, peeled and finely chopped
12 garlic cloves, minced
4 tbsp gochujang paste
1 litre beef stock
2 tsp sweet soy sauce
2 lemongrass stalks, bashed
1 tsp fish sauce
200g drained kimchi (reserve the juice), plus extra to serve
50ml kimchi juice from the jar
salt

Serving suggestion
white or black rice

1. Season your oxtail pieces all over with salt. Heat up a large stew pot on a medium-high heat and add the peanut oil. Once hot, add your oxtail and sear for 5 minutes, turning, until well browned all over (do this in batches, if necessary). Remove from the pot and set aside.

2. Add the onions to the pot and sauté for 5 minutes, until soft, then add the pimento berries, cumin seeds, coriander seeds and ginger and sauté for 2 minutes to soften. Reduce the heat to medium, add the garlic and gochujang paste and cook for 4 minutes, until soft and thick.

3. Tip the oxtail back into the pot and mix well. Add the beef stock, soy sauce, bashed lemongrass and fish sauce. Bring the liquid to the boil, cover the pot with the lid, reduce the heat and simmer for 2 hours, until the oxtail is almost tender.

4. Add the kimchi and kimchi juice and mix well. Part-cover the pot with the lid and simmer for 30 minutes, until the oxtail is tender. Serve with white or black rice and extra kimchi.

USA

CHILE COLORADO

SERVES
FOUR

I like to see this as a simplified version of the Mexican beef stew birria – it has a similar method but fewer ingredients. One of the best things about it is how the sauce thickens and attaches to the meat. The results are so warming and soothing, and work perfectly on a cold evening with rice, avocado and a beer.

PREP
20 MINS
plus marinating

COOK
2 HRS 10 MINS

800g beef shin, cut into 4cm cubes
2 tsp peanut oil
2 red onions, finely diced
1 red pepper, deseeded and finely diced
6 garlic cloves, minced
2 tsp tomato purée
2 tsp ground cumin
1 tsp red chilli powder
2 tsp sweet paprika
900ml beef stock
3 tsp dried oregano
½ tsp caster sugar
salt and black pepper

1 Season your beef shin pieces with a little salt and pepper, then set aside at room temperature to marinate for 1 hour before cooking.

2 Make the chilli paste. Bring a pot of water to the boil. Add all the chillies and boil for 10 minutes, until partially rehydrated, then turn off the heat. Add the tomatoes and leave the chillies and tomatoes to sit in the water for 10 minutes, until the chillies are fully rehydrated. Scoop out the chillies and tomatoes. When cool enough to handle, peel the skin from the tomatoes (it should slip off easily) and place the flesh in a blender with the chillies and a ladleful of the chilli water. Blitz to a smooth paste, then set aside.

3 Heat up a large stew pot on a medium-high heat and add the peanut oil. Once hot, add the beef and sear for 5 minutes, turning, until well browned on all sides (do this in batches, if necessary). Remove the meat from the pot and set it aside.

Pictured on page 126

CHILLI PASTE
4 dried ancho chillies, deseeded
10 dried guajillo chillies, deseeded
2 Roma tomatoes

4 In the same pot, add your onions and red pepper and cook for 5 minutes until soft. Add the garlic and tomato purée, reduce the heat to medium and cook for 2 minutes until the garlic is soft and the purée is thick. Now add the cumin, chilli powder and paprika and cook for 1 minute to cook out the spices.

5 Add the beef back to the pot and mix well. Place a sieve on the rim of the pot and pour in the chilli paste, leaving it to strain into the stew. Mix well and discard the contents of the sieve. Pour in the beef stock and add the oregano and sugar, then bring the liquid to the boil. Cover the pot with the lid, reduce the heat and simmer for 1 hour 45 minutes, until the beef is tender. Remove the lid and season with salt to taste. Serve with white rice, avocado, lime wedges and coriander.

Serving suggestions
white rice or flatbreads, avocado, lime wedges, fresh coriander

PORK & LAMB

KHORESH E KHALALT	130
HABICHUELAS	132
CHORIZO WHITE BEAN STEW	134
TUSCAN-STYLE BEAN STEW	136
SUNDUBU JIGAEE	138
RED BEANS LOUISIANA	140
PORT WINE STEW	142
SANCOCHO	144
TABAKH ROHO	148
FEIJOADA	150
BAMIA	154
GHORMEH SABZI	156
BROWN STEW LAMB	158
GOAT WATER	162
CHANFANA	164
LAMB TAGINE	166
NIHARI	168

IRAN

KHORESH E KHALALT

SERVES FOUR

This dish is a result of my deep love for Persian cuisine. It's a stand-out for me, and that's partly because of the barberries. One of my favourite berries, I eat them daily just as they are. They add a great sweetness to this stew, which is balanced so well by the tangy dried limes.

PREP
15 MINS
plus soaking

COOK
1 HR 45 MINS

4 Persian dried black limes
800ml boiling water, plus extra for the limes
1 tbsp sunflower oil
600g bone-in lamb shoulder, cut into 5cm cubes
1 onion, diced
1 small cinnamon stick
3 green cardamom pods, bashed
3 garlic cloves, minced
½ tsp ground turmeric
1 tsp ground black pepper
2 tbsp tomato purée
50g slivered almonds
30g dried barberries (or use dried cranberries or goji berries, if you can't find barberries)
3 tbsp Saffron Water (see page 211)
a pinch of ground cardamom
1 tsp rose water
salt

1. Pierce the dried limes carefully and place them in a bowl and just cover them with boiling water. Leave them to soak for 30 minutes before using.

2. Heat up a large stew pot on a medium-high heat and add the sunflower oil. Once hot, add the lamb and sear it, turning, for 5 minutes, until browned all over. Remove the meat from the pot and set aside.

3. Add the onion to the pot, reduce the heat and fry for 5 minutes, until soft. Add the cinnamon stick and cardamom pods, mix well and cook for 5 minutes, until fragrant. Add the garlic and soften for 1 minute, then add the turmeric and black pepper. Mix well, cook for a further few minutes, then stir in the tomato purée. Leave to cook for 5 minutes, until the purée turns a dark red colour, but is not burnt.

4. Add the lamb back to the pot, along with the soaked and drained dried limes, then add the 800ml of boiling water. Season with salt to taste, then bring the liquid to a simmer. Reduce the heat, cover the pot with the lid and cook for 1 hour, until the lamb is tender.

5. Add the slivered almonds, barberries (or cranberries or goji berries), saffron water, ground cardamom and rose water, then mix well and simmer, uncovered, for a further 20 minutes to let the flavours infuse and to bring the stew together. Serve with Persian tahdig.

Serving suggestion
Persian Tahdig (see page 203)

PUERTO RICO

HABICHUELAS

SERVES FOUR

A star of vibrant Puerto Rican cuisine, habichuelas boasts more than just flavour – it also reveals hints of Puerto Rico's colonial history, showing the Spanish influence through key elements such as the use of a sofrito, tomato sauce, olives and pork. I've really started to observe similarities between the Spanish and Latin American cuisines and it's made me realise that recipes are far more than just a collection of ingredients – they are a manifestation of complex history and influences.

PREP
10 MINS

COOK
30 MINS

1 tsp sunflower oil
120g smoked pancetta or back bacon, diced
1 tbsp garlic paste
2 tbsp Green Seasoning (see page 210)
180g passata
2 tsp dried oregano
1 x 100g Sazón Goya packet (with annatto)
400ml vegetable stock
1 x 400g can pinto beans, drained and rinsed
150g peeled and deseeded pumpkin flesh, cut into 3cm cubes
6 pitted green olives
1 tbsp juice from the olive jar
15g fresh coriander, leaves picked and chopped, plus extra to garnish
1 tbsp capers
2 tsp lime juice
salt

1. Heat a large stew pot on a medium heat and add the sunflower oil. Once hot, add the smoked pancetta or bacon and cook for 3 minutes, stirring often to prevent sticking, until the fat has rendered and the meat is browned all over. Add the garlic paste and green seasoning and cook, uncovered, for 5 minutes, until the liquid has almost gone from the green seasoning.

2. Add the passata, oregano, Goya seasoning and vegetable stock. Mix well and bring to the boil. Season with salt to taste.

3. Add the beans and pumpkin, cook for 15 minutes, uncovered, until the stew is thick, then add the olives, olive juice, coriander, capers and lime juice. Heat through for 5 minutes and then serve with white rice, fried plantain slices, sliced avocado, and sprinkled with extra coriander.

Serving suggestions
white rice, fried plantain slices, sliced avocado

SPAIN/PORTUGAL

CHORIZO WHITE BEAN STEW

SERVES
TWO

This hearty, Mediterranean stew was inspired by my years living in Spain and Portugal, where I had access to so many different kinds of chorizo. I loved experimenting with them, first in pasta sauces and then in stews. Eventually my favourite combination emerged – white wine and chorizo. For me, the sweetness of the white wine does an amazing job of balancing the smokiness of the chorizo.

PREP
10 MINS

COOK
45 MINS

2 tsp extra virgin olive oil
200g cooking chorizo, thinly sliced
80g leek, thinly sliced
½ onion, thinly sliced
2 garlic cloves, minced
50g sun-dried tomatoes in oil, drained and finely diced
2 tbsp tomato purée
75ml white wine
½ tbsp smoked paprika
1 tsp sweet paprika
100ml chicken stock
100g passata
1 x 400g can white beans, such as cannellini or butter beans, drained and rinsed
8 pitted green olives
20g flat-leaf parsley, leaves picked and chopped
salt

1. Heat a large stew pot on a medium-high heat and add the olive oil. Once hot, add the chorizo and fry for 3 minutes to render some of the fat. Remove the chorizo using a slotted spoon and set it aside on a plate. Add the leek and onion to the pot and sauté for 5 minutes, until soft.

2. Add the garlic and diced sun-dried tomatoes and soften for 2 minutes. Add the tomato purée, then cook on a medium heat for 3 minutes to develop that rich flavour. De-glaze the pot with the white wine and let it reduce by half (about 5 minutes), then add the chorizo back to the pot and season with the smoked and sweet paprikas.

3. Add the chicken stock and passata, then bring the liquid to a simmer. Simmer, uncovered, for 15 minutes, until the stew starts to reduce and thicken. Keep stirring to avoid anything sticking to the bottom of the pot.

4. Add the white beans and olives, then simmer them in the stew for 10 minutes to heat through. Season to taste with salt and finish with a sprinkling of the parsley. Serve with bread or rice.

Serving suggestions
bread or white rice

ITALY

SERVES FOUR

TUSCAN-STYLE BEAN STEW

Inspired by the Tuscan classic fagioli all'uccelletto, this is a classic summertime stew. During a trip to Tuscany, I ate some absolutely divine plates of food, including this one. It was served as a side dish to other meats (traditionally, game birds, hence the translation of its Italian name: 'beans of the little bird'). Imagine eating it my favourite way – with a glass of crisp, cold white wine and the warm Italian sun on your skin. There are few things – if any – that are better.

PREP 10 MINS **COOK** 50 MINS

2 tbsp extra virgin olive oil
1 tsp fennel seeds
500g Italian sausages, skin removed and sliced (regular sausages work just fine, if you can't find Italian)
2 onions, finely diced
8 garlic cloves, minced
4 tbsp tomato purée
240ml white wine
280g passata
480ml chicken stock
1½ tsp dried sage
2 x 400g cans cannellini beans, drained and rinsed
salt and black pepper

1. Heat a large stew pot on a medium heat and add the olive oil. Once hot, add the fennel seeds and toast them until fragrant (about 1 minute). Add the sausage slices and fry for about 5 minutes, stirring, until lightly browned, then add the onions and sauté for 5 minutes, until soft.

2. Add the garlic and tomato purée and cook for 5 minutes, until the purée turns a dark red colour, but is not burnt. Add the white wine to deglaze the pan and let it reduce by half (about 10 minutes).

3. Add the passata, chicken stock, sage and a pinch of pepper.

4. Bring the liquid to the boil and cover the pot with the lid. Reduce the heat, then simmer for 15 minutes. Taste and adjust the seasoning with salt, if necessary, then add the beans and mix well.

5. Simmer, uncovered, for 10 minutes, until the beans are warmed through. Season again with salt to taste, if needed, and serve with some bread or rice.

Serving suggestions
bread or white rice

KOREA

SUNDUBU JIGAEE

SERVES
TWO

A staple in Korean cuisine, kimchi is also a store-cupboard essential in my house – and my new favourite ingredient for a stew. It's a traditional Korean side dish, made from fermented cabbage infused with gochujang, ginger, garlic and much else besides, to create an umami-packed, lightly spiced and tangy flavour. It's so tasty and versatile – I've used it in absolutely everything you can think of, from eggs to salads. And now a pork and tofu stew.

PREP
10 MINS

COOK
1 HR 10 MINS

1 tbsp sunflower oil
300g pork belly, cut into 3cm cubes
2 tsp garlic paste
3 tsp gochujang paste
500ml vegetable stock
240g kimchi with juices
½ tsp fish sauce
1 tsp light soy sauce
400g extra-firm tofu, cut into 3cm cubes
2 eggs
1 spring onion, finely diced

1. Heat up a large stew pot on a medium-high heat and add the sunflower oil. Once hot, add the pork belly and sear it for 5 minutes, turning, until browned all over. Add the garlic paste and cook for 1 minute, then add the gochujang paste. Reduce the heat to medium and cook out the paste for 3 minutes.

2. Add the vegetable stock, kimchi and juices, fish sauce and soy sauce. Bring the liquid to the boil, cover the pot with the lid, reduce the heat to a simmer, then simmer the stew for 40 minutes, until the pork belly is tender.

3. Remove the lid and add the tofu. Simmer, uncovered, for 15 minutes, until the stew has reduced lightly and the tofu is cooked through. Crack the eggs into the middle of the stew and cook for a further 5 minutes, until the whites are set but the yolks are still runny. Sprinkle with the spring onion and serve in bowls with one egg on top of each portion and with rice.

Serving suggestion
white rice

USA

RED BEANS LOUISIANA

SERVES FOUR

A Louisiana classic – soft and creamy red beans are simmered in a rich and smoky Andouille sausage-based sauce, infused with fragrant Cajun spices, garlic, onions and celery. Each bite will transport you straight into the heart of New Orleans. Andouille sausage is a type of smoked pork sausage originating from France, seasoned with onion, garlic and spices to form a staple ingredient in Cajun and Creole cuisine. Of course, Andouille sausage is the most traditional and yields the best results but, honestly, whatever smoked sausage you can get hold of works amazingly!

PREP
10 MINS

COOK
2 HRS 30 MINS

plus overnight soaking

1 tsp sunflower oil
250g smoked Louisiana Andouille sausage, sliced (chorizo or polish smoked sausage also work well)
½ celery stick, finely diced
1 onion, finely diced
½ green pepper, deseeded and finely diced
200g dried red kidney beans, soaked overnight in water, then drained and rinsed
1.4 litres chicken stock
4 tsp Cajun seasoning
½ tsp cayenne pepper
2 tsp smoked paprika
2 tsp dried sage
2 tsp dried thyme
4 bay leaves
salt

Serving suggestion
white rice

1. Heat a large stew pot on a medium heat and add the sunflower oil. Once hot, add the sausage slices and sizzle for 2–3 minutes until some of the fat renders. Remove the sausage from the pot and set aside.

2. Tip the celery, onion and green pepper (the holy trinity) into the pot. Immediately season with salt, reduce the heat to medium-low and sauté for 10–15 minutes, until super-soft. Add the beans to the pot with the chicken stock, spices and herbs, then return the fried sausage to the pot. Bring the liquid to the boil, then reduce the heat, cover with the lid and simmer for 1 hour 30 minutes, until the beans are just tender enough to be mashed with a fork.

3. Remove the lid and leave the stew to bubble away for another 30–45 minutes, stirring occasionally, until it has thickened and the beans are cooked so that you can mash them easily with the back of a fork. Mash about one third of the beans in the stew, making the result nice and thick. Serve with rice.

PORTUGAL

PORT WINE STEW

SERVES FOUR

Since living in Portugal, I have become a huge lover of port – it is now my favourite drink. With that in mind, it would be wrong to write a stew book and not include it as a base for one of the recipes. Port brings a sweet element to this dish, which is balanced nicely with the flavours from the smoky chouriço.

PREP
10 MINS

plus overnight soaking

COOK
1 HR 30 MINS

100g Portuguese chouriço (or regular chorizo), sliced into 1cm rounds
300g boneless pork shoulder, cut into 4cm cubes
1 onion, finely diced
5 cloves
3 bay leaves
1 tsp cumin seeds
3 garlic cloves, minced
3 tbsp tomato purée
250ml port
200g dried black beans, soaked overnight in water, then drained and rinsed
1 litre boiling water
1 rosemary sprig
2 thyme sprigs
2 tsp dried sage
1 tsp mixed peppercorns
salt and black pepper

1. Heat up a large stew pot on a medium heat and add the chouriço. Fry for 2 minutes, stirring occasionally, until browned all over. Remove the chouriço from the pot and set aside. Add the pork shoulder to the pot and sear for 5 minutes, turning, until browned all over.

2. Add the onion, cloves, bay leaves and cumin seeds and mix well. Season with a pinch each of salt and pepper, then sauté for 5 minutes, until the onion is soft and the herbs and spices are aromatic.

3. Add the garlic and soften for 1 minute, then add the tomato purée and fry for 5 minutes, until the purée turns a dark red colour, but is not burnt. Then, go in with the port to deglaze the pan and leave it to bubble away until reduced by half (about 10 minutes).

4. Add the browned chouriço back to the pot along with the soaked black beans, boiling water, rosemary, thyme, sage and peppercorns. Season to taste with salt, then cover with the lid, reduce the heat and simmer for 45 minutes, until the beans are tender. Remove the lid and leave to cook, uncovered, for a further 20 minutes, to thicken it all up. Serve with rice.

Serving suggestion
white rice

CARIBBEAN

SANCOCHO

SERVES
FOUR

Sancocho is eaten all over the Spanish-speaking Caribbean islands, including Puerto Rico, Cuba and the Dominican Republic, as well as in Latin American countries such as Venezuela and Colombia. I've tried so many versions and, even though I've loved them all, my favourite comes from the Dominican Republic. In this recipe, though, I've fused them together, with touches of each version brought together in this recipe. It produces a super-comforting and hearty stew that is great for batching.

PREP
20 MINS
plus marinating

COOK
2 HRS 55 MINS

2 skinless chicken drumsticks
300g boneless pork shoulder, cut into 5cm cubes
150g pork ribs, cut into individual ribs
200g beef short ribs
2 tbsp white wine vinegar
1 lime, juiced
1 tsp salt
2 tbsp sunflower oil
1 tbsp caster sugar
800ml chicken stock
150g squash, peeled, deseeded and chopped into large cubes
150g cassava, peeled and chopped into large cubes
100g malanga (taro), peeled and chopped into large cubes
50g green plantain, peeled and sliced
100g corn-on-the-cob, cut into 4 slices

1. Make the marinade. Preheat your oven to 240°C/220°C fan. Put both peppers and the onion, garlic and celery into a non-stick, ovenproof dish and season with salt and pepper. Place the dish in the oven and roast the vegetables for 20 minutes, until charred and tender.

2. In the meantime, place all your meat in a large bowl with 1 litre of water and the white wine vinegar, lime juice and the 1 teaspoon of salt. Leave the meat in the liquid while the vegetables are roasting in the oven.

3. Tip the roasted vegetables into a blender or food processor along with the 1 teaspoon of salt, the olive oil, Worcestershire sauce, coriander, oregano and cumin. Pulse the mixture to a smooth paste – this is your marinade.

4. Remove the meats from the water, then pat them dry and place them in another large bowl. Pour the marinade over the top and marinate the meat for at least 1 hour – or ideally overnight, covered, in the fridge, for the best results. Don't discard the marinade left in the bowl. Give it a swill with some water and pour it into a small pot and keep it until you're ready to cook.

Pictured on page 146

MARINADE
½ green pepper, deseeded and chopped
½ red pepper, deseeded and chopped
1 large red onion, chopped
6 garlic cloves, peeled and left whole
1 celery stick plus a handful of leaves, roughly chopped
1 tsp salt, plus extra to season
1 tbsp olive oil
1 tbsp Worcestershire sauce
50g fresh coriander, leaves and stems
4 tbsp dried oregano
1 tbsp ground cumin
black pepper

5. Take your meat out of the fridge and let it come up to room temperature before cooking (30–60 minutes). Heat up a large stew pot on a medium-high heat and add the sunflower oil. Once hot, add the sugar and wait until it caramelises and turns a dark brown – but don't let it burn. If you let it go too far and it burns, you'll need to start again, as the stew will taste bitter.

6. Add your meat pieces to the caramel and sear, turning, for 4 minutes, until a lovely dark brown colour forms all over. Add your swilled marinade water to the pot, as well as the chicken stock, which should cover the meat. Bring the liquid to the boil, then reduce the heat, cover the pot with the lid, and leave the stew to simmer for 30 minutes, until the chicken is cooked through.

7. Remove the chicken pieces from the pot, to prevent them overcooking, and set them aside. Leave the remainder of the stew to simmer, with the lid on, for a further 1 hour 30 minutes, until the rest of the meats are tender.

8. Add the chicken back into the pot along with all the vegetables and simmer for a further 30 minutes, uncovered, until all the vegetables are cooked through. Season to taste with salt, then serve with rice and avocado.

Serving suggestions
white rice, avocado

SYRIA

TABAKH ROHO

SERVES
FOUR

Celebrating the dazzling flavours of the Levant region, this slow-braised lamb stew showcases Syrian home cooking. Don't be tempted to leave out the drizzle of pomegranate molasses at the end of the method. I have grown to love everything about pomegranate molasses. I first used it as a fancy cocktail ingredient in the pres I served up at university (my flatmates were big fans!). Then, I decided to integrate it into my cooking. In this stew, the really special thing is the combination of pomegranate and mint – a refreshing and tangy fusion of flavours. It's so moreish. I hope you love it as much as I do.

PREP
15 MINS

COOK
1 HR 40 MINS

2 tbsp olive oil
700g bone-in lamb or stewing lamb, diced (I like to use lamb shanks)
1 onion, finely diced
200g aubergine, cut into 2cm cubes
120g courgette, cut into 2cm cubes
2 tbsp tomato purée
1 tsp garlic paste
160g passata
2 tbsp ground black pepper, plus extra to season
¼ tsp ground cardamom
1 tsp Lebanese 7-spice (optional; see page 208)
2 tsp salt, plus extra to season
500ml chicken stock
6 small mint leaves, finely chopped, plus extra to garnish
2 garlic cloves, minced
2 tbsp pomegranate molasses

1. Heat up a large stew pot on a medium-high heat, then add the olive oil. Once hot, add the lamb and season with some black pepper, then sear for 5 minutes, turning, until browned all over (do this in batches, if necessary). Remove the lamb and set it aside on a plate. Reduce the heat to medium, add the onion to the pot and sauté for 5 minutes, until soft.

2. Add the aubergine and courgette. Sauté for 5 minutes, until soft, then add the lamb back to the pot along with the tomato purée and garlic paste and cook for a further 3 minutes. Add the passata, measured black pepper, ground cardamom, Lebanese 7-spice (if using), measured salt and chicken stock. Bring the liquid to the simmer, cover the pot with the lid and simmer for 1 hour, until the lamb is tender.

3. Add the mint, garlic and pomegranate molasses. Mix well and leave the stew to simmer with the lid off until it has thickened, about 20 minutes. Taste and adjust the salt levels as needed. Serve with vermicelli rice or white rice, garnished with a few extra mint leaves.

Serving suggestions
Vermicelli Rice (see page 206) or white rice

BRAZIL

FEIJOADA

SERVES
FOUR

This was one of the first stews I made, while filming my series Stews from Around the World. The intense flavour comes from the carne seca (dried beef) and linguiça calabresa (spicy sausages) – staples of Brazilian cuisine. For me, carne seca, in particular, is non-negotiable – you can find it on Amazon, or in Brazilian grocery stores, and it's well worth the effort. As this is a very rich stew, it goes perfectly with toasted cassava flour (farofa), greens and oranges, which not only give a genuine flavour of Brazil, but balance out the intensity.

PREP
15 MINS
plus overnight soaking

COOK
3 HRS

1 tbsp sunflower oil
6 garlic cloves, minced
5 bay leaves
250g dried black beans, soaked overnight in water, then drained and rinsed
100g Brazilian carne seca (see intro), soaked overnight in water
75g smoked back bacon rashers, diced
100g pork belly, cut into large cubes
150g pork ribs, cut into individual ribs
125g linguiça calabresa sausages, sliced (found in Brazilian stores; or use chorizo)
2 tsp ground cumin

Serving suggestions
farofa, orange slices, collard greens or kale, white rice

1. Put a large stew pot on a medium-high heat and add the sunflower oil. Once hot, add the garlic and bay leaves. Sauté for 1 minute, then add the rehydrated black beans and 1.8 litres of water. Bring the water to the boil, then reduce the heat, cover the pot with the lid and simmer the beans for 1 hour, until tender.

2. With 20 minutes to go on the beans, bring a separate pot of water to the boil. Add the carne seca, and boil it for those 20 minutes, then drain – this will remove some of the excess salt from the rehydrated meat. Set aside.

3. Meanwhile, sear the meats. Put a large frying pan on a medium-high heat. First, add your bacon pieces and fry for 2 minutes, until lightly browned, then remove from the pan, leaving some of the fat behind. Add the pork belly cubes to the pan and sear them, turning, for 5 minutes, until browned all over. Remove them from the pan and repeat, in turn, with the ribs and the sausages or chorizo. Set all the meats aside.

4. Once the hour is up, remove the lid from the stew pot and add in all the meats (including the carne seca) and the cumin, then cover again and cook for a further 1 hour, until the meats are cooked through and tender. Using the back of a fork, mash about one third of the beans to thicken the stew. Leave the pot uncovered and cook the stew for a further 30 minutes to 1 hour, until it has reduced and thickened to your liking. Serve with farofa, orange slices, greens and rice.

MIDDLE EAST

BAMIA

SERVES
TWO

The preparation of bamia (okra and meat – in this case, lamb – stew) varies throughout the Levant region and I'd say my version attempts to blend them all. Adding Lebanese 7-spice (also called baharat, a blend of spices that usually includes cinnamon, cloves, coriander, cumin, pepper, nutmeg and sweet paprika) represents a touch of Lebanon, while the garlic and basil celebrates the Palestinian preparation, for example. Seeing as I just couldn't decide on my favourite, single version, fusing them seemed the best of all worlds.

PREP
10 MINS

COOK
1 HR 40 MINS

4 tbsp olive oil
300g bone-in lamb or stewing lamb, diced (I like to use lamb shanks)
1 onion, diced
1 tsp Lebanese 7-spice (optional; see page 208)
2 cinnamon sticks
½ tsp ground cardamom
2 tsp tomato purée
500ml chicken stock
160g passata
4 bay leaves
10 okra, sliced
a squeeze of lemon juice or 1 tsp white wine vinegar (optional)
6 garlic cloves, minced
6 basil leaves
salt

1. Heat up a large stew pot on a medium-high heat, then add 2 tablespoons of the olive oil. Once hot, sear your diced lamb, turning, for 5 minutes, until browned all over (do this in batches, if necessary). Reduce the heat to medium, then add the onion and sauté for 3 minutes, until softened. Add the 7-spice and the cinnamon sticks, and cook for a further 2 minutes, until fragrant.

2. Add the ground cardamom and cook for 2 minutes, then add the tomato purée. Cook for 3 minutes, then add the chicken stock, passata and bay leaves. Put the lid on the pot and simmer the stew for 1 hour, until the lamb is almost tender.

3. Meanwhile, if you don't want the slimy texture, put the okra slices in a large bowl of water made acidic with the squeeze of lemon juice or teaspoonful of white wine vinegar. Leave the okra to sit in the water for 30 minutes.

4. Remove the lid from the pot, add the okra slices (drained, if necessary) and simmer the stew, uncovered, for 20 minutes, until the okra is tender.

5. Meanwhile, heat the remaining 2 tablespoons of olive oil in a small frying pan. Add the garlic and basil and fry for 2 minutes, until fragrant. Add this to the stew, cook for a further 5 minutes, to infuse, then season well with salt to taste. Serve with rice.

Serving suggestions
Vermicelli Rice (see page 206) or white rice

IRAN

GHORMEH SABZI

SERVES FOUR

One of my favourite ingredients is Persian black dried limes – limes that have been boiled in salt water, then left to dehydrate. They are a staple ingredient in Iran and other Gulf countries, and added to sauces and stews, they pack a powerfully fragrant punch of concentrated citrus. I use them in far more than Persian cooking – in fact, I'll put them in any dish that requires a citrus element, adding them into the pot to work their magic (I also like to bite into them whole – try it if you're feeling brave). Here, in this ghormeh sabzi from Iran, the dried limes are the backbone of the dish.

A side note before you begin: the herby mixture for this stew has to be very finely chopped for it to work well. You can use a food processor to speed things up, if you like.

PREP
20 MINS

plus overnight soaking

COOK
1 HR 45 MINS

50g chives, very finely chopped
100g fresh coriander, leaves and stems very finely chopped
300g flat-leaf parsley, leaves and stems very finely chopped
100g spinach leaves, very finely chopped
4 spring onions, green parts only, very finely chopped
3 tbsp extra virgin olive oil
½ tsp saffron strands
1 litre chicken stock, plus 6 tbsp for the saffron
6 Persian dried black limes
2 tbsp sunflower oil
1kg bone-in lamb or stewing lamb, diced (I like to use lamb shanks)
2 onions, diced
2 tsp ground turmeric
1 tsp ground black pepper
8 garlic cloves, minced
160g dried red kidney beans, soaked overnight in water, then drained and rinsed
½ tsp dried fenugreek leaves, crushed
salt

1 Combine the chives, coriander, parsley, spinach and spring onions in a bowl. Heat up a frying pan or skillet on a medium heat and add the olive oil. Add the herb mixture, reduce the heat, mix well and cook it for 20 minutes, stirring frequently to avoid burning, until the mixture starts to turn really dark green – this will give the stew its authentic colour. Once you see that green, scoop out the mixture from the pan and set aside.

2 Meanwhile, in a pestle and mortar, grind down your saffron strands. Add the 6 tablespoons of chicken stock to the mortar and mix well until the saffron has fully dissolved. Let it sit for 20 minutes. Pierce the dried limes carefully and place them in a bowl, then just cover them with boiling water. Leave them to soak for 30 minutes before draining and using.

3 Now we can start the stew. Heat up a large stew pot on a medium-high heat and add the sunflower oil. Once hot, add the lamb pieces and sear, turning, for 5 minutes, until browned all over. Add the onions, then immediately season with a sprinkle of salt and add the turmeric. Mix well and cook, covered with the lid, for 5 minutes, until the onions have softened and there is liquid in the pot.

4 Add the black pepper and garlic and cook for 2 minutes, then add the beans and mix them into the contents of the pot.

5 Add the crushed fenugreek, the litre of chicken stock, the herb mixture and the dried limes. Bring the liquid to a simmer, then cover the pot with the lid and cook for 15 minutes. Add the saffron stock and mix well. Taste and adjust the salt levels as needed. Replace the lid on the pot and simmer for a further 1 hour, until the lamb is tender and the beans are cooked through. Serve with Persian tahdig and salad.

Serving suggestions
Persian Tahdig (see page 203), salad

JAMAICA

BROWN STEW LAMB

SERVES
FOUR

This Jamaican dish is a true celebration of Caribbean culinary craftsmanship. Browning the sugar before adding the meat is a common cooking method throughout the Caribbean islands – it adds such a rich flavour and balances out the spicy elements.

PREP
20 MINS
plus marinating

COOK
2 HRS

2 limes, juiced
¼ tsp salt, plus extra to season
1kg bone-in lamb or stewing lamb, cut into 5cm cubes
2 tbsp sunflower oil
1 tbsp caster sugar
600ml chicken stock
6–10 thyme sprigs
2 tbsp Green Seasoning (optional; see page 210)
1 potato, peeled and chopped into 3cm cubes
200g cassava, peeled and chopped into 3cm cubes

1. Pour about 1 litre of cold water into a large bowl. Add the lime juice and measured salt, then add the lamb, turning it to coat. Let it sit for 30 minutes in the fridge, so that the lamb can tenderise by absorbing some of the salt water.

2. Scoop the lamb from the bowl of seasoned water and place it in another large bowl. Add all the dry spices and herbs for the marinade and stir to combine, making sure each piece of lamb is well coated with all the seasonings, then add the rest of the marinade ingredients and mix. Leave to sit for at least 2 hours, or preferably overnight, covered, in the fridge. Bring up to room temperature before cooking (30–60 minutes).

3. To start the stew, heat up a large pot on a medium-high heat and add the sunflower oil. Once hot, add the caster sugar and stir frequently, until the sugar starts to bubble and turn a dark brown, but is not burnt. If the sugar burns, your stew will taste bitter, so you'll need to discard the contents of the pot and start again.

4. Add the lamb pieces (excluding the vegetables from the marinade but keep them to one side) to the pot and sear over medium-high heat for 5 minutes, turning, until browned all over. Reduce the heat to medium, cover the pot with the lid and cook for 8 minutes so that the lamb releases its liquid. Remove the lid to check that the liquid has developed in the pot. Turn up the heat again and simmer fiercely until about 70% of the liquid has gone (about 5–10 minutes).

Pictured on page 160

MARINADE
24 pimento (allspice) berries
2 tsp ground white pepper
2 tsp garlic powder
4 tsp dried thyme
6 cloves
2 tsp ground pimento (allspice)
1 tsp cayenne pepper
1 tsp red chilli powder
1 tsp ground ginger
2 tsp sweet paprika
2 tsp dried marjoram
1 tsp ground black pepper
1 tsp salt
4 tbsp sunflower oil
2 tsp red pepper paste
1 tsp tomato purée
30g fresh ginger, peeled and minced
12 garlic cloves, minced
½ red pepper, deseeded and sliced
½ green pepper, deseeded and sliced
½ yellow pepper, deseeded and sliced
1 onion, sliced
2 spring onions, green parts only, diced
2 small celery sticks with leaves, sliced
2 tomatoes, sliced

Serving suggestions
Rice and Peas (see page 202),
fried plantain slices

5   Add the remaining ingredients from the marinade bowl to the pot and cook for 5 minutes to soften. Meanwhile, add the chicken stock to the marinade bowl and mix well to get all the remaining marinade off the sides. Pour this liquid into the stew pot and bring to the boil. Add the thyme and green seasoning (if using), then reduce the heat, cover the pot and simmer for 1 hour, until the lamb is cooked through and tender.

6   Taste the stew and season with more salt, if you wish. Add the potato and cassava and simmer, uncovered, for 25 minutes to thicken the stew. Serve with rice and peas and fried plantain.

MONTSERRAT

GOAT WATER

SERVES FOUR

Coming from my family's home island of Montserrat, in the West Indies, for me this goat water is more than just a stew – it's personal. I first travelled to Montserrat in 2024 and it was arguably one of the most incredible trips of my life. I got to experience my island with my own two eyes after years of hearing about it. While I was there, my favourite thing to eat was goat water, our national dish. Massive shoutout to Betsy and Cherise from the Montserrat Tourist Board for showing me how it's done, so that I could develop my own version when I got back home to England.

PREP
15 MINS

plus soaking

COOK
2 HRS 50 MINS

1.5kg bone-in goat, cut into large chunks
1 tsp salt
1 lemon, juiced
1 tbsp white wine vinegar

STEW
1 onion, finely diced
2 large spring onions, green parts only, finely diced
6 garlic cloves, minced
25 thyme sprigs
1 tbsp dried rosemary
25 cloves
10 pimento (allspice) berries
1 tbsp dried marjoram
2 tbsp adobo (badia)
4 tbsp plain flour
½ tbsp ground black pepper
1 tbsp gravy browning (for the colour)

1. Tip the goat chunks into a large mixing bowl and add the salt, lemon juice and white wine vinegar, then pour over enough cold water to cover the meat. Let the meat soak for 20 minutes (to quickly brine the meat), then drain.

2. Put a large stew pot on a high heat. Pour in 2.5 litres of water, then once the water is boiling, add the drained goat meat and simmer for 10 minutes, skimming off the scum that rises to the surface. Once you have removed all the scum, cover the pot with a lid, reduce the heat, and simmer the meat for 20 minutes.

3. Add all the stew ingredients to the pot, except the flour, black pepper and gravy browning. Season to taste with salt, then mix well and simmer, with the lid on, for 2 hours, until the goat is almost tender.

4. Once the 2 hours are up, remove 1 cupful of the stew liquid and pour it into a large bowl. Gradually whisk in the flour until well combined and smooth. If you want the stew to be even thicker, you can add more flour.

5. Add the black pepper, then, little by little, add the mixture back into the stew along with the gravy browning. This will thicken the stew nicely. Leave the stew to cook, uncovered, for a further 20 minutes to fully cook out the flour. Serve with some fresh bread.

Serving suggestion
bread

PORTUGAL

CHANFANA

SERVES FOUR

While I was living in Portugal, so many local friends told me that I had to make a chanfana. So I did. It's a brilliant one-pot wonder – you combine all the ingredients, then pop it in the oven, leave it for a couple of hours, and you're good to go. Beware, though: your neighbours may be knocking on the door asking for a cheeky bowl or two. It smells delicious and good smells travel…

PREP
10 MINS

plus marinating

COOK
2 HRS 30 MINS

- 1kg bone-in lamb or goat shoulder, cut into large chunks
- 2 onions, sliced
- 8 garlic cloves, sliced
- 200g smoked bacon or pancetta, diced
- 40g flat-leaf parsley, leaves picked and chopped
- 10 cloves
- 6 bay leaves
- 2 tbsp smoked paprika
- 4 tbsp sweet paprika
- 2 tsp ground black pepper, plus extra to season
- 2 tsp salt, plus extra to season
- 2 rosemary sprigs or 2 tbsp dried rosemary
- 750ml red wine
- 30g unsalted butter or lard

1. An hour before you intend to start cooking, generously season your chosen meat with salt and pepper, then set it aside, covered, in the fridge until you're ready. Bring it up to room temperature before cooking (30–60 minutes).

2. Preheat your oven to 200°C/180°C fan. Combine all the remaining ingredients in a large, ovenproof stew pot. Add the meat, making sure it's submerged (if it's not, use water to top up as necessary), then place the pot into the oven with the lid on and cook the meat for 1 hour.

3. Remove the pot from the oven, taste for salt and pepper levels, adjusting as necessary. Place the pot back in the oven with the lid in place and cook for a further 1 hour 30 minutes, until the meat is fall-apart tender. (Alternatively, you can cook this entirely on the hob instead of in the oven: place the pot on a medium-low heat and follow the same timings.) Serve with boiled new potatoes and cabbage or kale.

Serving suggestions
boiled new potatoes, boiled cabbage or kale

MOROCCO

LAMB TAGINE

SERVES
FOUR

24 HRS

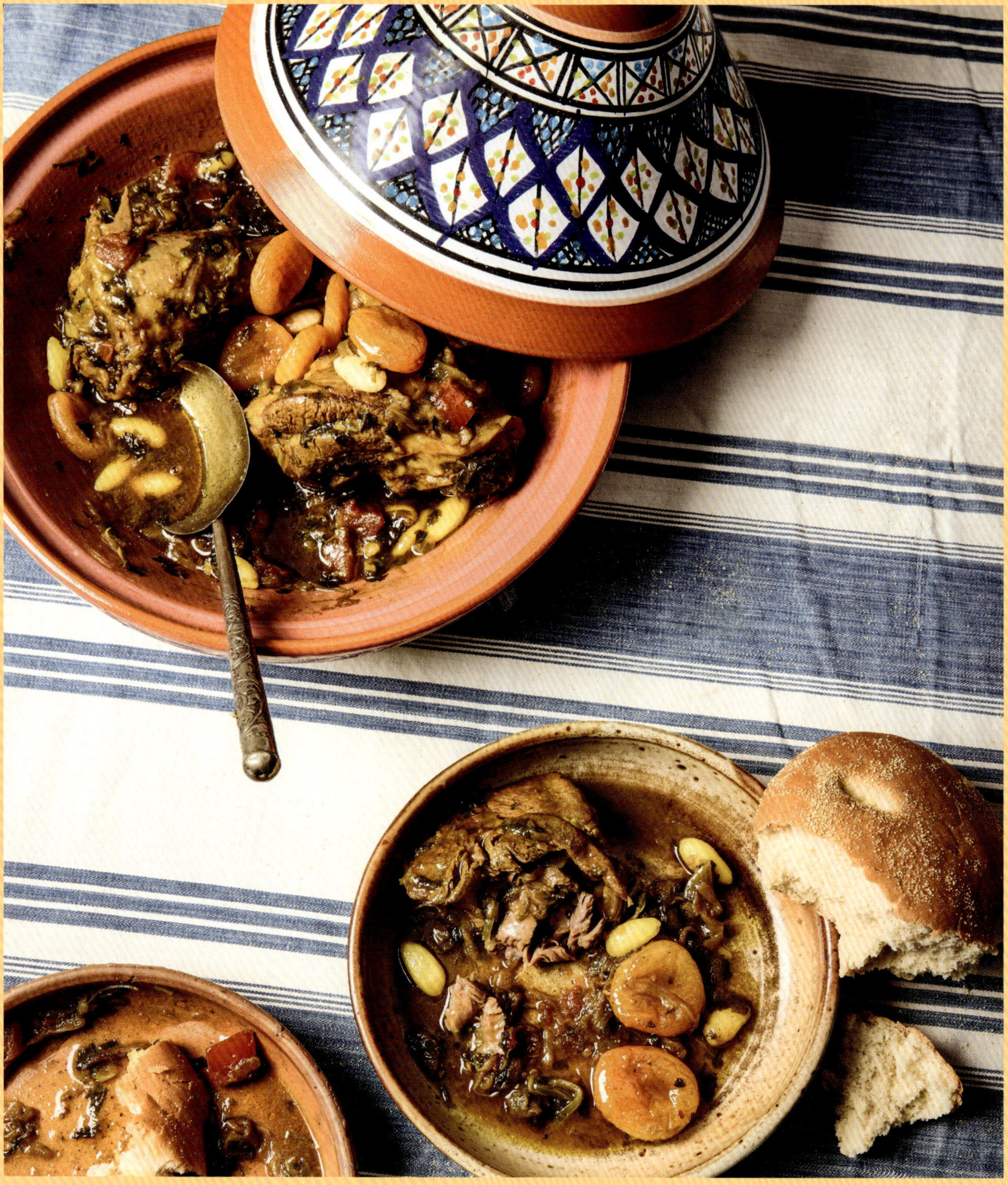

In 2023, in a town called Midalet in Morocco, something really special happened – this stew. I was in a restaurant and the waiter brought out this steaming tagine. As soon as the waiter removed the lid, my senses went into overload. Then, I dipped in my bread and knew straight away that this was perhaps going to be the best thing I would ever have eaten. The meat was so tender and flavourful – it was an absolutely surreal experience.

PREP
15 MINS
plus marinating

COOK
2 HRS

4 lamb shanks
30g unsalted butter
2 tbsp extra virgin olive oil
2 red onions, sliced
½ tsp salt
1 tbsp caster sugar
3 garlic cloves, minced
1 large Roma tomato, chopped
15g fresh coriander sprigs
20g flat-leaf parsley sprigs
¼ tsp saffron strands mixed with 2 tbsp warm water

MARINADE
3 tbsp extra virgin olive oil
1 tsp sea salt
2 tsp Ras el Hanout (see page 209)
1 tsp ground turmeric
2 tsp ground cumin
½ tsp ground ginger
1 tsp cayenne pepper
1 tsp ground black pepper

TOPPING
50g blanched whole almonds
5 tbsp rose water
1 tsp caster sugar
100g blanched dried apricots

Serving suggestion
Moroccan round bread

1. Make the marinade by combining all the marinade ingredients in a large bowl with 2 tablespoons of water. Mix well into a paste.

2. Add your lamb shanks to the bowl with the marinade and turn them in the marinade so that they are completely covered. Cover the bowl and leave the shanks to marinate in the fridge for at least 30 minutes – you'll get the best results if you can leave them overnight. (Bring to room temperature before cooking.)

3. In a large stew pot or hob-safe tagine, heat up the butter and olive oil on a medium-low heat. Once hot, add the onions, salt and sugar, then cover the pot or tagine with the lid and leave the onions to cook for 30 minutes, until caramelised. This stew is all about moisture, so it's important to keep as much of it as possible in the pot (avoid the temptation to lift the lid!).

4. After the 30 minutes, add the minced garlic. Leave it to cook for 1 minute, then add the marinated lamb shanks, followed by the tomato, coriander and parsley. No need to mix – just let them do their thing.

5. Pour 100ml of water into the marinade bowl to collect the rest of the marinade. Mix well, then add this to the pot along with the saffron water, turn up the heat and bring the liquid to a simmer. Then, reduce the heat, cover the pot or tagine with the lid again and cook for 1 hour 30 minutes (if using a regular pot, add a dash more water – a tagine will work just as it is, as it creates a steam that cooks everything so well), until the lamb is tender and you are left with a wonderful stew at the bottom of the pot or tagine.

6. Meanwhile, make the topping. Place a frying pan on a low heat and add the almonds. Pour in the rose water and sugar and cook for 5 minutes, until the sugar has dissolved and the almonds are coated. Remove from the heat and set aside until the stew has finished cooking.

7. Spoon a portion of the almond mixture over each shank and sprinkle with the apricots. Serve with Moroccan round bread.

NIHARI

PAKISTAN

SERVES FOUR

This Pakistani classic originates from the Mughal Empire and it is truly a dish to warm your soul. When I first made it, I couldn't believe the delicious smells that filled my kitchen – they totally blew me away. Do try to get atta flour, if you can – it's a chickpea flour and, added 30 minutes before the stew is ready, it not only thickens it but provides a really soft and warming flavour that I love. It really brings the dish together.

PREP
15 MINS

COOK
2 HRS 45 MINS

- 1 tbsp ghee or unsalted butter
- 4 lamb shanks
- 1 onion, finely diced
- 4 garlic cloves, minced
- 10g fresh ginger, peeled and minced
- 1 tsp caraway seeds
- 3 bay leaves
- 1 star anise
- ½ tsp ground turmeric
- ½ tsp red chilli powder
- 2½ tbsp nihari masala
- 800ml chicken stock
- 25g atta or gram flour
- salt
- flat-leaf parsley leaves, to garnish

1. Preheat the oven to 190°C/170°C fan. Heat up a large ovenproof stew pot on a medium heat and add the ghee or butter. Once melted and hot, add your lamb shanks and sear them for 5 minutes, turning, until browned all over. Add the onion, garlic, ginger, caraway seeds, bay leaves and star anise, then sauté for 5 minutes, until the onion and garlic are soft.

2. Sprinkle in the turmeric, red chilli powder and the nihari masala, mix well and cook for 2 minutes to cook out the spices. Add the chicken stock, bring the liquid to the boil, then cover the pot with the lid. Transfer the pot to the oven and cook for 2 hours, until the lamb is tender. Open the oven, carefully remove the pot and place it on a heatproof surface. Remove the lamb shanks from the pot and set them aside.

3. Heat a frying pan on a medium heat. Add the atta or gram flour and lightly toast it for 1 minute, until fragrant. Tip the toasted flour into a large, heatproof bowl, add 4 ladlefuls (150ml per ladle) of the broth from the pot, then mix well until there are no lumps. Spoon the mixture back into the pot and return the lamb shanks. Cover and place the pot back into the oven to cook for a further 30 minutes, until the flour has been cooked out. Season to taste with salt, then serve each shank with the broth spooned over, sprinkled with parsley, and with Indian flatbreads on the side.

Serving suggestion
Indian flatbreads, such as naan

SEAFOOD

MARMITAKO	**172**
CAJUN PRAWN STEW	**174**
CALDEIREDA DE PIEXE	**176**
MOQUECA	**178**
STEWED SALTFISH	**180**
THAI PRAWN STEW	**182**
ENCEBOLLADO	**184**
GHALIEH MEYGOO	**186**
FISKGRYTA	**188**
CIOPPINO	**190**
MALDIVIAN TUNA STEW	**192**
ARROZ DE MARISCO	**194**
SEA BASS TAGINE	**196**

SPAIN

MARMITAKO

SERVES FOUR

The Basque Country in northern Spain, with its beautiful mountains, dramatic coastline and vast, sandy beaches, offers many delights – and one of them is marmitako, a lightly spiced and refreshing tomato-based stew using fresh tuna. I first tasted fresh tuna not in Spain but in the Maldives. That experience and, subsequently, this dish have transformed my perception of tuna as the claggy stuff of primary-school lunches to a perfect protein for a flavourful, but simple stew.

PREP 15 MINS

COOK 55 MINS

2 tbsp olive oil
1 red pepper, deseeded and diced
1 Spanish white onion, diced
6 garlic cloves, sliced
140g cherry tomatoes, sliced
100g sun-dried tomatoes, chopped
2 bay leaves
2 tbsp tomato purée
100g passata
800ml fish stock
2 tsp sweet paprika
2 small potatoes, peeled and cut into 2cm cubes
400g skinless tuna fillet, cut into 3cm cubes
20g flat-leaf parsley, leaves picked and chopped
salt and black pepper

1. Heat a large stew pot on a medium heat and add the olive oil. Once hot, add the red pepper and onion, and sauté for 5 minutes, until soft. Add the garlic, cherry tomatoes, sun-dried tomatoes and bay leaves, then mix well, cover the pot with the lid and cook for 5 minutes, until soft.

2. Remove the lid and add the tomato purée. Cook, uncovered, for 5 minutes, until the purée turns a dark red colour, but is not burnt. Add the passata and fish stock, then the sweet paprika, and then season with salt and pepper to taste. Cover the pot with the lid and simmer for 20 minutes to allow the flavours to infuse.

3. Remove the lid, add the potatoes and simmer, uncovered, for 15 minutes, until the potatoes are cooked. Finally, add the tuna and simmer for 5 minutes, until cooked through. Serve in bowls, scatter over the parsley and enjoy just as it comes.

USA

SERVES
FOUR

CAJUN PRAWN STEW

Cajun was one of the first spices I started to use as a student – I chose it for its versatility, knowing that I could use it in multiple dishes and get great results. My favourite option was to use it in a creamy Cajun pasta – my weekly student staple in my fresher year! Now, it underpins this creamy, roux-based stew. You can never get bored of Cajun…

PREP
15 MINS

COOK
40 MINS

400g shelled and deveined raw prawns
½ tsp salt, plus extra to season
7 tsp Cajun seasoning
80ml sunflower oil
80g plain flour
1 large onion, finely diced
½ large celery stick, finely diced
½ large green pepper, deseeded and finely diced
600ml fish stock
½ tsp cayenne pepper
½ tsp ground black pepper

1. Pat dry the prawns, then place them in a large bowl. Sprinkle over the measured salt and 2 teaspoons of the Cajun seasoning and mix very well. Set aside while you start the stew.

2. Heat up a large stew pot on a medium heat and add the oil. Leave the oil to heat a little bit, then add the flour and slowly mix them together to make a roux. Cook on a medium heat for around 15 minutes, stirring very frequently to avoid clumping, until the roux is a dark brown colour, but is not burnt. If the roux burns, start over again, otherwise the stew will taste bitter.

3. Add the onion, celery and green pepper, stir them into the roux and cook for about 5 minutes, or until the vegetables are soft, then gradually – a little at a time – mix in the fish stock. Once all the fish stock is in, season with the remaining Cajun, the cayenne pepper and black pepper, then mix well. Taste and season with salt as needed. Cover the pot with the lid and simmer for 10 minutes, until the flavours have incorporated.

4. Remove the lid and add the seasoned prawns. Cook, uncovered, for 3–5 minutes, or until the prawns are fully cooked through. Serve with rice.

Serving suggestion
white rice

PORTUGAL

CALDEIREDA DE PIEXE

SERVES FOUR

 45 MINS

Historically, I was never very big on fish stews, but living in Portugal completely changed that for me. During one warm day in October, I went to my local market in Porto and found some beautiful fresh fish. I asked the fishmonger how I could turn it into a stew and she told me to make a caldeireda. We all have her to thank!

PREP
30 MINS

COOK
12 MINS

500g skin-on, firm white fish fillets (such as monkfish), cut into 5cm pieces
1 large onion, finely sliced
1 large red pepper, deseeded and sliced crossways into rings
5 garlic cloves, minced
1 large green pepper, deseeded and sliced crossways into rings
2 large tomatoes, sliced into rounds
1 small potato, peeled and sliced
10g flat-leaf parsley, leaves picked and finely chopped, plus 30g leaves and stems, chopped, for the liquid
300ml fish stock
75ml white wine
25ml white wine vinegar
100g passata
1 tsp smoked paprika
½ tsp sweet paprika
1 tsp garlic powder
salt and black pepper

Serving suggestion
crusty white bread

1. Season your fish pieces with some salt and pepper to taste, then set aside.

2. Take a large stew pot and layer the ingredients as follows: half the onion goes first, followed by half each of the red pepper, garlic, green pepper, tomatoes and potato. Then layer on all the fish. Repeat the vegetable layers one more time to use them up and finish off with the 10g of parsley leaves.

3. Add all the remaining ingredients to a large jug, mix well, then season to taste with salt.

4. Place the pot on a medium-high heat and pour in the spiced liquid from the jug. Cover the pot with the lid and bring the liquid to the boil. Once boiling, reduce the heat and simmer for 12 minutes, until the fish is cooked through. Serve with some fresh, crusty white bread.

BRAZIL

MOQUECA

SERVES FOUR

This is Brazil's statement seafood stew – vibrant and refreshing, using minimal ingredients. I find that it harmonises a perfect balance of rich, tangy and warming flavours, and transports me to everything I imagine a Brazilian beach to be.

PREP
20 MINS
plus marinating

COOK
20 MINS

- 150g skinless, boneless white fish fillets, cut into 5cm pieces
- 2 limes, juiced
- ¼ tsp salt, plus extra to season
- 1 tsp olive oil
- 200ml coconut milk
- 200ml fish stock
- ½ tsp garlic powder
- 2 tsp smoked paprika
- 1 tsp sweet paprika
- 1 tsp sustainable palm oil
- 1 onion, sliced
- 3 garlic cloves, sliced
- 1 tomato, thinly sliced
- ½ red pepper, deseeded and thinly sliced
- ½ green pepper, deseeded and thinly sliced
- ½ yellow pepper, deseeded and thinly sliced
- 150g shelled and deveined raw prawns
- 25g fresh coriander, leaves picked and chopped

1. In a large bowl, mix together the white fish, the juice of one of the limes, the measured salt and the olive oil. Cover the bowl with cling film or foil, then set aside in the fridge for at least 15 minutes, or up to 1 hour.

2. In a jug, mix together the coconut milk, fish stock, garlic powder and smoked and sweet paprikas, then season to taste with salt. Set aside.

3. Place a large stew pot on a medium heat, then add the palm oil. Once hot, add the onion and sauté for 5 minutes, until soft. Then, add the garlic and soften for 1 minute.

4. In layers, add half the sliced tomato and half of each of the peppers to the pot – do not mix. Layer the white fish on top, then finish with further layers of the remaining tomato and peppers.

5. Pour over the coconut milk and fish stock mixture, turn up the heat and bring the liquid to the boil. Cover the pot with the lid and cook for 8 minutes, until the fish is cooked through. Remove the lid and add the prawns and half of the chopped coriander. Make sure the prawns are submerged, then simmer for 3–5 minutes, until the prawns are fully cooked through.

6. Squeeze over the juice of the remaining lime and sprinkle in the remaining coriander. Mix well and then season again to taste with salt. Serve with white rice and lime wedges for squeezing over.

Serving suggestions
white rice, lime wedges

CARIBBEAN

SERVES FOUR

STEWED SALTFISH

I've brought together various versions of saltfish stew for this recipe – it appears in so many different forms all over the West Indies. Mostly, though, this dish is inspired by my nan's saltfish, which we'd have at her house on a Sunday for breakfast, with bakes (Caribbean fried dumplings) and fried plantain. It's family comfort cooking at its best.

PREP
30 MINS

COOK
1 HR

400g dried saltfish (chunks or strips)
½ tbsp coconut oil
1 onion, sliced
5 pimento (allspice) berries
2 bay leaves
½ small red pepper, deseeded and sliced
½ small green pepper, deseeded and sliced
½ small yellow pepper, deseeded and sliced
½ small orange pepper, deseeded and sliced (optional)
5g fresh ginger, peeled and minced
4 garlic cloves, minced
1 Roma tomato, sliced
6 thyme sprigs
1 tsp dried marjoram
½ tsp ground black pepper
¼ tsp cayenne pepper
¼ tsp ground turmeric
200g peeled and deseeded squash or pumpkin, cut into 2cm cubes
200ml coconut milk
250ml fish stock
1 tsp fish sauce
1 spring onion, green part only, chopped
salt

1. Start by removing the saltfish from the packet and placing it in a large pot of boiling water. Boil it for 15 minutes, remove the fish from the water and rinse it. Repeat this one more time with fresh boiling water, to remove the excess salt. Alternatively, you can leave the fish to soak overnight in cold water, which will do the same job. Drain and set aside.

2. Put a large stew pot on a medium heat and add the coconut oil. Once melted and hot, add the onion and a pinch of salt and sauté for 5 minutes, until soft. Add the pimento berries and bay leaves and cook for 2 minutes, until fragrant.

3. Add all the peppers and cook for 5 minutes, until soft and fragrant. Then, add the minced ginger and garlic and soften for 2 minutes. Add the tomato, thyme, marjoram, black pepper, cayenne and turmeric, cover the pot with the lid and cook for 5 minutes, until the tomato starts to break down.

4. Add the squash or pumpkin, coconut milk, fish stock and fish sauce. Cover again with the lid, reduce the heat and simmer for 15 minutes, for the flavours to fully develop.

5. Remove the lid and simmer for a further 10 minutes. Finally, add the spring onion and saltfish to the pot and cook, still uncovered, for 15 minutes, until it is cooked through. Serve with bakes and fried plantain.

Serving suggestions
Bakes (see page 212), fried plantain slices

THAILAND

THAI PRAWN STEW

SERVES
FOUR

When I was a child, Thai red curry was one of my favourite meals. Now that I'm older, I realise just how versatile an ingredient Thai red curry paste is. I use it all the time: in soups, eggs, stews and even pasta. My favourite use, though, is to put it in a stew and let it work its magic. This one is perfect – umami from the mushrooms, sourness from the citrus of the lemongrass and lime leaves, zingy freshness from the lime juice and creamy coconut to balance the spice of the paste. Wonderful.

PREP
10 MINS

COOK
35 MINS

2 tbsp coconut oil
1 onion, diced
15g fresh ginger, peeled and minced
4 garlic cloves, minced
2 tbsp red Thai curry paste
1 lemongrass stalk, bashed
200ml coconut milk
4 makrut lime leaves
500ml fish stock
1 tsp fish sauce
1½ tsp light soy sauce
a pinch of caster sugar
160g chestnut mushrooms, thinly sliced
75g kale, sliced
300g shelled and deveined raw prawns
10g fresh coriander, leaves picked and chopped
salt

1. Heat up a large stew pot on a medium heat and add the coconut oil. Once melted and hot, add the onion and sauté for 5 minutes, until soft. Add the minced ginger and garlic and cook for 2 minutes to soften.

2. Add the red Thai curry paste and cook for 5 minutes, until fragrant, then add the bashed lemongrass stalk, followed by the coconut milk, lime leaves, fish stock, fish sauce, soy sauce and sugar. Mix well and bring the liquid to the boil. Cover the pot with the lid, reduce the heat and simmer for 10 minutes, until the stew is fragrant.

3. Add the mushrooms, then replace the lid and leave them to simmer in the stew for 5 minutes to soften. Add the kale and simmer with the lid on for 5 minutes, until wilted.

4. Add the prawns and leave them, uncovered, to simmer for 3–5 minutes, until fully cooked through. Remove the lemongrass stalk, then taste for salt, adjusting as needed. Finally, stir in the coriander. Serve in bowls with white rice and lime wedges for squeezing over.

Serving suggestions
white rice, lime wedges

ECUADOR

SERVES FOUR

ENCEBOLLADO

This iconic coastal dish from Ecuador is a wonderful balance of comfort and heat – comfort from the earthy cassava and rich, savoury broth and heat from my favourite Sazón Goya seasoning. The tuna chunks become tender to perfection as they simmer away in all that goodness.

PREP
20 MINS

COOK
45 MINS

2 red onions, peeled
1 tbsp sunflower oil
½ red pepper, deseeded and diced
½ green pepper, deseeded and diced
60g leek, white part only, sliced
3 garlic cloves, minced
5g fresh ginger, peeled and minced
1 tomato, sliced
½ x 100g Sazón Goya packet (with annatto)
½ tbsp dried oregano
700ml fish stock
½ tsp red chilli powder
15g fresh coriander, leaves picked and stalks reserved
100g cassava, peeled and cut into rough chunks
400g skin-on tuna fillet, cut into 3cm chunks
½ lime, juiced
salt and black pepper

1. Thinly slice one of the red onions and place it in a bowl of cold water, then set aside and leave it to soak (this removes some of the acidity) while you make the stew. Dice the other red onion and set aside.

2. Heat a large stew pot on a medium-high heat and add the sunflower oil. Once hot, add the diced red onion, both peppers and the leek. Sauté for 2 minutes, to soften a little, then add the garlic and ginger and soften for 1 minute. Add the tomato and cook, covered with the lid, for 10 minutes, until the tomato has broken down.

3. Add the Goya seasoning, oregano and fish stock. Bring the liquid to the boil. In a separate bowl, mix together the chilli powder with 50ml of water, then add that to the pot with the coriander stalks. Reduce the heat, cover the pot with the lid and simmer for 20 minutes, until all the flavours are incorporated.

4. Meanwhile, bring a separate large pot of water to the boil. Add the cassava and boil the chunks for 25 minutes, until tender. Drain them and then when the chunks are cool enough to handle, cut them into thin strips and set aside.

5. Add the tuna to the stew pot and let it simmer with the lid on for 10 minutes, until just cooked. Remove the fish from the pot. Skin the tuna and set the fish aside. Discard the coriander stalks from the stew. Pour the sauce into a blender and blitz until smooth. Pass the sauce through a fine-mesh sieve into a warmed jug (this will make it extra-fine). Season to taste with salt and pepper and stir through the lime juice. Set aside.

6. Remove the red onion slices from the water and drain. Now place the tuna and cassava in a serving bowl, then pour the sauce on top and sprinkle over the sliced red onions and the coriander leaves to serve.

SEAFOOD

IRAN

GHALIEH MEYGOO

SERVES TWO

Persian cuisine is one of my favourites. I started to really fall in love with it in 2023, when I tried the iconic Ghormeh Sabzi and Fesenjan stews. I was mesmerised by the unique and magical flavours. Indulge in the bustling flavours of Iran with this Persian prawn stew. Juicy fresh prawns are simmered in a fresh, tangy and rich sauce made from coriander, garlic, tamarind and fenugreek. A simple yet mouthwatering dish, which leaves you wanting more after every bite.

PREP
10 MINS

COOK
30 MINS

300g shelled and deveined raw prawns
2½ tsp ground turmeric
2 tbsp tamarind paste
300ml boiling water
1 tbsp sunflower oil
1 onion, diced
1 tsp fenugreek seeds
4 garlic cloves, minced
80g fresh coriander, chopped
4 tsp dried fenugreek leaves
½ tsp ground white pepper
a pinch of caster sugar
salt and black pepper

1. Tip the prawns into a bowl and sprinkle over 1 teaspoon of the turmeric. Season with salt and pepper and turn to coat the prawns in all the seasoning. Set aside.

2. Combine the tamarind paste in a heatproof bowl with the boiling water. Set aside until ready to use.

3. Heat up a large stew pot on a medium heat and add the sunflower oil. Once hot, add the onion and sauté for 3 minutes until almost soft, then add the fenugreek seeds. Mix well, frying them for 2 minutes, until fragrant.

4. Add the garlic and soften for 1 minute, then add the coriander and fenugreek leaves and mix very well. Pour in the tamarind mixture, then add the remaining turmeric and the white pepper, season to taste with salt and pepper, reduce the heat to low and leave the stew to simmer for 20 minutes, covered, until fully cooked.

5. Add the pinch of sugar to balance the flavour of the tamarind, then season the stew for a final time with some salt. Add the seasoned prawns and cook for 3–5 minutes, until the prawns are fully cooked through. Serve with rice.

Serving suggestions
white rice or Persian Tahdig (see page 203)

FISKGRYTA

SWEDEN

SERVES FOUR

This Scandinavian, creamy fish stew, flavoured with classic dill, reminds me of a childhood favourite – my mother's fishcakes. She would always start by simmering the fish in a cream and dill sauce, before making the patties and frying them into deliciousness. So, as much as fiskgryta is definitely of Scandinavian origin, this one has my memories of childhood sewn in, too.

PREP 15 MINS   **COOK** 45 MINS

10g unsalted butter
1 tbsp olive oil
80g leek, finely diced
1 onion, finely diced
2 tbsp tomato purée
3 garlic cloves, minced
150ml white wine
2½ tbsp dried dill or 20g fresh dill, tender fronds picked and finely chopped
150ml double cream
450ml fish stock
150g skinless salmon fillets, cut into 2cm cubes
250g skinless, firm white fish fillets, cut into 2cm cubes
150g peeled and deveined raw prawns
½ lemon, juiced
10g flat-leaf parsley, leaves picked and roughly chopped
salt and black pepper

1. Heat up a large stew pot on a medium heat. Once hot, add the butter and olive oil. When the butter has melted, add the leek and onion and a pinch of salt and sauté for 5 minutes, until soft.

2. Increase the heat to medium-high. Add the tomato purée and garlic and cook for 3 minutes, then add the wine to deglaze the pot and let it bubble away until reduced by half (about 10 minutes). Add the dill and double cream, then mix well to incorporate everything together.

3. Pour the fish stock into the pot, bring to the boil, then cover the pot with the lid and cook for 10 minutes. Remove the lid, taste the stew and season with salt and black pepper.

4. Add the salmon and white fish to the pot, then cover with the lid again, and cook the fish for 10 minutes. Add the prawns and leave the lid off, cooking for 3–5 minutes, until all the fish is fully cooked through. Stir through the lemon juice, sprinkle with the parsley and serve with boiled new potatoes.

Serving suggestion
boiled new potatoes

USA

CIOPPINO

SERVES FOUR

A herbaceous seafood stew, known for its bold flavours, this is San Franciscan comfort food at its coastal best. I love the lightness of this stew – it feels really easy to eat, but still packs plenty of flavour. The reduced white wine gives it a lovely, subtle sweetness, then the herbs ignite it with a burst of zesty freshness.

PREP
10 MINS

COOK
45 MINS

1 tbsp olive oil
1 onion, finely diced
1 tsp fennel seeds
2 garlic cloves, finely diced
1 tbsp tomato purée
200ml white wine
200ml fish stock
200g passata
1½ tbsp dried oregano
1 tbsp dried thyme
250g skinless firm white fish fillets (such as monkfish), cut into chunks
200g shelled and deveined raw prawns
½ lemon, juiced
15g fresh parsley, chopped
salt

1. Heat up a large stew pot on a medium heat and add the olive oil. Once hot, add the onion with a pinch of salt and sauté for 5 minutes, until soft. Add the fennel seeds and cook for 1 minute, until fragrant.

2. Add the garlic and tomato purée, increase the heat to medium-high and sauté for 5 minutes, until the purée is a dark red colour, but is not burnt. Add the white wine to deglaze the pot, then leave it to bubble away until it's reduced by half (about 10 minutes).

3. Add the fish stock, passata, oregano and thyme and season with salt to taste. Mix well and bring the liquid to the boil. Cover the pot with the lid, reduce the heat and simmer for 10 minutes, until fragrant.

4. Add the white fish pieces, cover the pot again and simmer for 10 minutes. Then, add the prawns and simmer, this time uncovered, for 3–5 minutes, until everything is cooked through. Finish off with the lemon juice and chopped parsley, and salt to taste. Serve with herby garlic bread.

Serving suggestion
herby garlic bread

MALDIVES

MALDIVIAN TUNA STEW

SERVES
TWO

I've got a crazy story behind this stew. On a hot, lazy afternoon in the Maldives, I met a super-amazing and friendly Dutch family. I spent the afternoon swimming, snorkelling and chatting with them and they invited me on a fishing trip – the idea was to catch some fish, then have our catch cooked by a local chef. How could I say no?! On that trip, we caught tuna and mahi mahi, which the chef later turned into so many delicious dishes, including the star of the show – this Maldivian-style tuna stew. It blew my mind! And, now, here it is made immortal in the book.

PREP
10 MINS

COOK
55 MINS

- 1 tbsp coconut oil
- ½ tsp cumin seeds
- ⅛ tsp yellow mustard seeds
- ¼ tsp fenugreek seeds
- 1 onion, diced
- 3 garlic cloves, minced
- 5g fresh ginger, peeled and finely chopped
- 1 tsp tomato purée
- 5 fresh curry leaves (or use dried, if necessary)
- ½ tsp ground turmeric
- 1 tsp curry powder
- ¼ tsp cayenne pepper
- 200ml coconut milk
- 300ml fish stock
- 1 pandan leaf
- ½ tsp fish sauce
- 400g skinless tuna fillets, cut into 3cm chunks

Serving suggestion
white rice

1. Heat up a large pot on a medium heat and add the coconut oil. Once melted and hot, add the cumin, mustard and fenugreek seeds and leave them to sizzle in the oil for 30 seconds. Add the onion, garlic and ginger and sauté for 5 minutes, until the onion is soft. Add the tomato purée and curry leaves and cook for a further 2 minutes, then add the turmeric, curry powder and cayenne pepper and mix very well. Cook out the spices for another minute.

2. Stir in the coconut milk, fish stock, pandan leaf and fish sauce. Mix well and bring the liquid to a light simmer. Part-cover the pot with the lid, reduce the heat and leave the stew to simmer for 40 minutes, until aromatic.

3. Add the tuna and leave it to simmer in the stew, uncovered, for 5–6 minutes to cook through. Serve with rice.

MEDITERRANEAN

SERVES FOUR

ARROZ DE MARISCO

Carolino rice is a Portuguese risotto rice, which makes it perfect as the backdrop for this Mediterranean seafood stew. It was one of the first authentic dishes I learned to make while living in Portugal – a brothy, seafood rice dish, quite like Spanish arroz caldoso, which is a similar dish, but far more brothy. The Portuguese version is slightly simpler – traditionally with no saffron, although I use it here – and is finished with lemon and fresh herbs.

PREP
15 MINS

COOK
50 MINS

1 tbsp olive oil
80g leek, finely diced
1 onion, finely diced
¼ red pepper, deseeded and finely diced
¼ green pepper, deseeded and finely diced
1 rosemary sprig, leaves picked and finely chopped
5 thyme sprigs, leaves picked and finely chopped
2 garlic cloves, minced
1 tbsp tomato purée
350ml white wine
½ tsp sweet paprika
1 tsp smoked paprika
50g passata
3 tbsp Saffron Water (see page 211)
100g Carolino rice (you can also use arborio or risotto rice)
800ml hot fish stock
400g prepared mixed seafood of your choice (such as prawns, clams and mussels)
½ tsp finely grated lemon zest
½ lemon, juiced
15g flat-leaf parsley, finely chopped
salt

1. Heat up a large stew pot on a medium heat and add the olive oil. Once hot, add the leek and onion and season with a pinch of salt. Sauté for 5 minutes, until soft, then add the red and green peppers. Sauté for a further 5 minutes, until soft.

2. Add the rosemary, thyme and garlic, then mix well and soften for 1 minute. Add the tomato purée, then cook for 5 minutes, until the purée turns a dark red colour, but is not burnt.

3. Pour in 150ml of the white wine to deglaze the pot, then leave it to bubble away until reduced by half (about 10 minutes). Add the sweet and smoked paprikas and the passata and mix well. Add the saffron water, reduce the heat to medium-low and cook for 2 minutes, until fragrant and well incorporated.

4. Add the rice to the pot and mix very well. One ladleful at a time, add the hot fish stock, stirring the rice as you go. Keep adding the stock as the previous ladleful is absorbed until you've added it all. This should take around 15 minutes and by now the rice should be fully cooked. Add your prawns and steam with the lid on for 3–5 minutes, until the prawns are cooked through.

5. Meanwhile, if you're using clams and mussels, heat a large frying pan or skillet over a medium heat, add the clams and mussels and the remaining white wine, then cover the pot with the lid and steam for 8–10 minutes, until the shellfish has opened (discard any that hasn't). Add the cooked clams and mussels to the stew.

6. Add the lemon zest and lemon juice to the pot and then serve, sprinkled with the fresh parsley.

MOROCCO

SEA BASS TAGINE

SERVES TWO

I had my first ever fish tagine in the magical coastal city of Essaouira in Morocco. As it arrived at the table, the smell was enough for me to know that I was about to eat something really special – a spiced sauce with tender vegetables and succulent, locally caught fish. The following day, I bought a load of ingredients at the local market and went to the sand dunes with my portable gas stove and videographer and filmed the exact stew. It was so good! Once I got home, I started adding my own twists – preserved lemons, rose harissa and saffron – so this is my version of a North African delight.

PREP 25 MINS

COOK 35 MINS

plus marinating

- 150g shelled and deveined raw king prawns
- 250g skinless sea bass fillets
- 1 tbsp olive oil
- 1 onion, thinly sliced
- 1 potato, peeled and sliced into 1.5cm rounds
- ½ red pepper, deseeded and sliced crossways into rings
- ½ yellow pepper, deseeded and sliced crossways into rings
- 1 tomato, sliced
- 450ml boiling water
- 8–10 pitted green olives
- 2 tbsp brine from the olive jar
- 1 lemon, juiced

1. Combine all the ingredients for the marinade, except the preserved lemon skin, in a large bowl. Add the prawns and sea bass to the bowl, turn to coat them in the marinade, then set them aside for at least 20 minutes or, covered, for up to 12 hours in the fridge.

2. Heat a large stew pot or hob-safe tagine on a medium heat, then add the olive oil. Layer the ingredients in the pot or tagine: start with the onion, followed by the potato, peppers, tomato and the preserved lemon skin. Remove the fish and prawns from the marinade and set them aside. Add the boiling water to the marinade bowl and mix well.

3. Pour the loosened marinade over the vegetables in the pot or tagine, then cover with the lid and simmer on a medium-low heat for 20 minutes, until the vegetables are becoming tender.

Pictured on page 198

MARINADE
3 tbsp rose harissa paste
2 preserved lemons, pulp and skin separated, skin diced
3 tbsp juice from the preserved lemon jar
2 tbsp brine from the olive jar
1 tbsp olive oil
15g flat-leaf parsley, leaves and stems chopped, plus extra to serve
15g fresh coriander, leaves and stems chopped, plus extra to serve
1½ tsp ground turmeric
1½ tsp ground coriander
½ tsp cayenne pepper
½ tsp smoked paprika
2 tsp ground cumin
1 tsp ground ginger

4 Add the sea bass on top of the vegetables, add the olives and brine, then re-cover the pot or tagine and cook for a further 10 minutes. Add the prawns, cover again and cook for a further 3–5 minutes, until all the fish and all the vegetables are fully cooked through.

5 Remove the lid, sprinkle over some extra chopped parsley and coriander and season with the lemon juice to serve.

SIDES & SPICES

RICE AND PEAS	**202**
PERSIAN TAHDIG	**203**
VERMICELLI RICE	**206**
WAAKYE RICE	**207**
LEBANESE 7-SPICE	**208**
RAS EL HANOUT	**209**
GREEN SEASONING (SOFRITO)	**210**
SAFFRON WATER	**211**
BAKES	**212**
TOSTONES	**213**

RICE AND PEAS

SERVES EIGHT

A form of rice and peas is eaten all over the Caribbean, with different versions depending on which island you are on. Jamaica's version is a hearty and creamy red kidney bean-based rice dish cooked in coconut milk and infused with bold Caribbean spices such as pimento, thyme and black pepper, and – if you're feeling brave – a Scotch bonnet. It's a dish that really embodies the warmth, comfort and flair of Jamaican home cooking.

PREP
10 MINS

plus overnight soaking

COOK
2 HRS 15 MINS

- 1 tbsp coconut oil
- 1 onion, roughly chopped
- 3 spring onions, green parts only, roughly chopped
- 10g fresh ginger, peeled and finely minced
- 5 garlic cloves, minced
- 200g dried red kidney beans, soaked overnight in water (or for at least 2 hours), then drained and rinsed
- 1.2 litres boiling water
- 8 thyme sprigs
- 4 tsp pimento (allspice) berries, freshly ground
- 1 tsp black peppercorns, freshly ground
- 1 tsp Worcestershire sauce
- 2 tsp light soy sauce
- 1 whole Scotch bonnet (optional)
- 400ml coconut milk
- 550g white basmati rice, washed
- salt

1. Heat up a large stew pot on a medium heat and add the coconut oil. Once melted and hot, add the onion, spring onions, ginger and garlic and fry for 2 minutes, until fragrant and soft. Add the soaked kidney beans, the boiling water, thyme sprigs, ground pimento, ground black pepper, Worcestershire sauce, soy sauce and Scotch bonnet (if using). Bring the liquid to a simmer, reduce the heat, cover the pot with the lid and cook for 1 hour 30 minutes, or until the kidney beans are cooked to fork tender.

2. Remove the thyme stalks and the Scotch bonnet (if using) from the pot and discard, then pour in the coconut milk and season generously with salt to taste. Once you're happy with the salt levels, add the washed basmati rice, then simmer with the lid on, on a low heat, for 15 minutes, by which time the rice should be almost cooked through.

3. Remove the pot from the heat and leave it just as it is, with the lid on, to steam for a further 15 minutes (don't touch it yet – this is an important step so that the rice can absorb all the moisture). Open the lid and fluff up the rice with a fork, then cover for a further 10 minutes, until each grain is fully cooked through. Serve.

PERSIAN TAHDIG

SERVES FOUR

A truly prized delicacy in Persian cuisine, the word tahdig in Farsi translates as 'bottom of the pot', where done right, you will see an irresistibly crispy layer of golden rice, as an end result of slow and delicate cooking. The tahdig is a labour of love which takes patience, care and skill. Long-grain basmati rice grains are par-boiled, then steamed until fluffy and aromatic. Prior to steaming, oil, saffron and turmeric are added to the bottom of the pan to bring out that golden glow for which the tahdig is so famously known.

PREP
10 MINS

plus soaking

COOK
1 HR

2 bay leaves
2 green cardamom pods
2 cloves
350g white basmati rice, soaked in cold water for 1 hour, then drained
2 tbsp rapeseed oil
3 tbsp Saffron Water (see page 211)
½ tsp ground turmeric
salt

1. Bring a large stew pot of water to a vigorous boil on a high heat. Add the bay leaves, cardamom pods and cloves and season with salt. Reduce the heat and simmer for 2 minutes, until fragrant. Add the drained rice and cook for 6 minutes, until par-boiled but not cooked through. Drain the rice, discarding the bay and spices, and rinse through with cold water under a tap. Set aside.

2. Heat up a very good non-stick pot on a medium-high heat, then add the rapeseed oil, half the saffron water and the ground turmeric and mix well. Once the oil starts to lightly smoke, add the part-cooked rice and spread it out in an even layer over the entire pot. Immediately use the back of a spoon to make 5 indents in the rice and scatter over the remaining saffron water. Cook, uncovered, for 5 minutes, until you start seeing some steam coming from the rice. Reduce the heat to medium-low, cover with a clean tea towel and then with a lid, and let it all steam like this for 40 minutes, until the rice is fully cooked through.

3. To flip out the tahdig, remove the pot from the heat and take off the lid. Place a large plate over the rice to fully cover, then quickly flip the pot, inverting the tahdig on to the plate. You should now have a beautiful, golden brown, crispy layer uppermost. Don't worry if it hasn't worked perfectly the first time you try – a perfect tahdig relies on trial and error (the quality of the non-stick pot and the intensity of the heat under the pot will make a big difference), but with practice you'll get there.

SIDES & SPICES

VERMICELLI RICE

SERVES TWO

A beloved staple across Middle Eastern and Mediterranean cuisines – where the pairing of long-grain rice and vermicelli noodles comes together to create a light, nutty and fluffy side dish for any great stew.

PREP
5 MINS

COOK
40 MINS

1 tbsp sunflower oil
50g dried vermicelli noodles
200g long-grain white rice, washed
450ml chicken or vegetable stock
salt

1. Heat up a large stew pot on a medium-high heat and add the sunflower oil. Once hot, add the vermicelli and fry for 2 minutes, or until lightly browned.

2. Add the rice and fry for 30 seconds until fragrant, then add the chicken or vegetable stock and season with salt to taste. Bring the liquid to a light simmer, reduce the heat to low, then cover the pot with the lid and cook for 15 minutes, until the rice is almost cooked.

3. Remove the pot from the heat and, without removing the lid, leave it to stand for 10 minutes, then remove the lid and fluff up the rice mixture with a fork. Cover with the lid again and leave to steam for a further 10 minutes, until everything is cooked through. Serve.

WAAKYE RICE

SERVES TWO

A dish rooted in comfort, culture and tradition, waakye rice embodies a distinctly earthy and comforting bowl of rice, typically served with Waakye Stew (see page 32). Black-eye peas are stewed down alongside sorghum (waakye) leaves until soft and tender. You are left with a beautifully dark red broth which you then bathe your rice in, until fluffy and tender.

PREP
10 MINS
plus overnight soaking

COOK
1 HR 20 MINS

1 litre boiling water
200g dried black-eye peas, soaked overnight in water, then drained and rinsed
10 sorghum leaves
1 tsp garlic powder
1 tsp ground black pepper
1 chicken or vegetable stock cube
200g white basmati rice, washed
salt

1. Make a stock. Place a large stew pot on a high heat, then add the boiling water and adjust the heat so that it's at a simmer. Add the beans and sorghum leaves, then reduce the heat, cover the pot with the lid and cook the beans and leaves for 45 minutes, until you have a dark red colour and the beans are fully cooked. Scoop out the beans and discard the sorghum leaves. Measure out 400ml of the stock and pour it into a separate large pot (discard the remainder).

2. Place the pot of stock on a medium heat and add the garlic powder, black pepper and crumbled stock cube, then season with salt to taste. Add the beans and basmati rice, reduce the heat to low, cover the pot with the lid and cook for 15 minutes, until the rice is almost cooked through.

3. Remove the pot from the heat and, without removing the lid, leave the rice to steam for a further 10 minutes. Remove the lid, fluff up the rice with a fork, then replace the lid and leave the rice to steam for a further 10 minutes, until all the grains are fully cooked through. Serve.

SIDES & SPICES

LEBANESE 7-SPICE

MAKES
3 TABLESPOONS

The heartbeat of Lebanese cooking, 7-spice – or baharat – is a blend of various spices, such as allspice, cloves and nutmeg, which forms a versatile and daily essential across the Levant region.

PREP
10 MINS

COOK
1 MIN

3 tsp pimento (allspice) berries
6 cloves
2 tsp cumin seeds
3 tsp coriander seeds
1 tsp ground cinnamon
½ tsp ground ginger
¼ tsp ground nutmeg
1 tsp ground coriander
1 tsp ground cumin
2 tsp ground cardamom

1. Heat a frying pan on a medium-high heat. Once hot, add the pimento berries, cloves and cumin and coriander seeds and toast for about 30 seconds, until fragrant. Tip the spices on to a plate to stop them cooking and leave them to cool. Once cool, tip them into a spice blender or mortar, along with all the ground spices and pulse, or grind with the pestle, until the mixture is as smooth and fine as it can be. Store in an airtight jar.

MAKES
3 TABLESPOONS

RAS EL HANOUT

'Head of the shop' in Arabic, this versatile spice blend is a household staple across the Maghreb. Common ingredients include cumin, coriander, green cardamom and turmeric, with multiple variations existing throughout the region. It can be used to enrich anything from stews to soups. The end result is a fine fusion of bold, earthy and sweet flavours to level up absolutely any dish.

PREP
10 MINS

COOK
1 MIN

2 green cardamom pods
3 cloves
5 pimento (allspice) berries
1 tsp cumin seeds
1 tsp coriander seeds
½ small cinnamon stick
1 tsp ground turmeric
¼ tsp ground nutmeg
½ tsp ground ginger
½ tsp ground white pepper
1 tsp ground black pepper
½ tsp flaky sea salt

1. Heat a frying pan on a medium-high heat. Once hot, add the cardamom pods, cloves, pimento berries, cumin and coriander seeds and cinnamon stick and toast for about 30 seconds, until fragrant. Tip the spices on to a plate to stop them cooking and leave them to cool. Once cool, tip them into a spice blender or mortar, along with all the ground spices, both peppers and the salt and pulse, or grind with the pestle, until the mixture is as smooth and fine as it can be. Store in an airtight jar.

MAKES
400ML

GREEN SEASONING (SOFRITO)

Caribbean green seasoning is the backbone to numerous wonderful delights of the region. Each island has its own version, which varies from house to house. The essential base involves a herbaceous, fragrant and aromatic sauce, containing an array of fresh greens and herbs, including, thyme, garlic, onions and peppers, which are blended alongside oil and citrus until you have a powerful jar of bright green goodness.

PREP
10 MINS

20g flat-leaf parsley, leaves and stems
40g fresh coriander, leaves and stems
3 spring onions, green parts only
1 onion, cut into quarters
2 celery sticks, cut in half
5g fresh ginger, peeled
6 garlic cloves, peeled but left whole
1 red pepper, deseeded
1 green pepper, deseeded
2 Scotch bonnets, deseeded (optional, depending on your preference for heat)
3 tbsp vegetable oil
2 limes, juiced
salt

1. Place all the ingredients, including salt to taste, in a blender and pulse until the mixture is smooth and combined. Transfer the mixture to an airtight container. It will refrigerate for up to 5 days, or keep for up to 3 months in the freezer. Use as required (if frozen, defrost before use).

SAFFRON WATER

MAKES
150ML

A powerful elixir made with an ingredient also known as the world's most valuable spice. Saffron threads are steeped in boiling water, which allows the extraction of that vibrant orange colour and earthy taste, which is then used us a wonderful flavour booster across the Middle East, India and Morocco.

PREP
5 MINS

Plus standing

2 tsp saffron strands
150ml boiling water

1. Grind down the saffron strands into a fine powder using a pestle and mortar, then tip into a heatproof bowl, add the boiling water and mix well. Leave to stand for at least 20 minutes before using. Store in an airtight jar in the fridge for up to 1 week.

BAKES

SERVES FOUR

Caribbean bakes – also known as Johnny cakes in the Virgin Islands or floats in Guyana – are soft, fluffy and versatile pieces of fried bread which are a staple across the Caribbean. The dough is made with a simple set of ingredients, including flour, salt and baking powder, and then fried until golden and crispy. I serve them with my Stewed Saltfish (see page 180).

PREP
25 MINS

COOK
15 MINS

250g plain flour
1 tsp baking powder
¼ tsp salt
½ tsp sugar
150ml lukewarm water
1 tbsp unsalted melted butter
500ml vegetable oil

1. Mix together all the dry ingredients in a large bowl until well combined. Slowly add the lukewarm water, alongside the melted butter, then gently knead until you form a dough with a slightly sticky consistency and not too firm. Cover the bowl with a clean tea towel and leave the dough to rest for 15 minutes.

2. Divide the rested dough into small equal-sized portions, then roll each portion between your palms into a ball. Leave the balls to rest for a further 10 minutes. Now place each ball on a floured surface and roll out into a flat circle, using a rolling pin.

3. Heat up a heavy-based frying pan on a medium-high heat, then add the vegetable oil and slowly heat it up. Once hot, add the dough discs, in batches, and fry until they puff up and begin to brown on one side, about 2 minutes, then flip and cook until brown on the other side.

4. Remove and place on a cooling rack to drain any excess oil while you fry the remaining bakes.

TOSTONES

SERVES FOUR

A wonderfully golden, crispy, tasty snack of fried, smashed and fried-again green plantains, which is a popular delicacy eaten throughout the Caribbean and Latin America. Unlike sweet plantains, the green ones offer a more savoury element, which complements a range of stews.

PREP 10 MINS

COOK 20 MINS

500ml vegetable oil
4 green plantains
salt

1. Heat up a heavy-based frying pan on a medium-high heat, then add the vegetable oil and slowly heat it up.

2. In the meantime, prepare your plantains by peeling them and discarding the skins. Slice the plantains into equal 2.5cm pieces.

3. Once the oil is hot, add the plantain slices and fry for 4 minutes on each side until lightly browned and soft on the inside.

4. Remove from the pan with a slotted spoon or fish slice and smash gently with the bottom of a cup to flatten each slice into a rough circle. Then place them back into the pan and fry for a further 2 minutes on each side until golden and crispy.

5. Remove and place on a cooling rack to drain any excess oil, then season to taste with a sprinkle of salt and serve.

SIDES & SPICES

INDEX

Note: page numbers in **bold** refer to illustrations.

adzuki bean 38
Afghanistan 42
Africa
  North 58
  West 46
aji de gallina 92–3, **92**
almond 167
apricot (dried) 167
arroz de marisco 194–5, **194**
aubergine
  chickpea maafe 46
  ciambotta 20
  daube 56
  khoresh gheymeh 22
  tabakh roho 148

bacon
  beef bourguignon 98, **99**
  chanfana 164, **165**
  feijoada 150, **151–3**
  habichuelas 132, **133**
  jardineira 102, **103**
bakes **180**, 212
bamia 154, **155**
banana (green) 36
bean(s) 41–62
  chilli con carne 96
  chorizo white bean stew 134, **135**
  daube 56
  fasolia 62
  feijoada 150
  ghormeh sabzi 157
  habichuelas 132
  harissa black-eye peas 58
  Ital stew 60–1
  jackfruit and tarragon stew 38
  jardineira 102
  loubia 44
  port wine stew 142
  puca picante 30
  qorma a lubia 42
  red beans 52, **53**
  red beans Louisiana 140, **141**

  rice and peas 202
  stew peas 51
  Tuscan-style bean stew 136, **137**
  see also chickpea(s)
beef 95–125
  beef bourguignon 98, **99**
  bo kho 118, **119**
  chile Colorado 124–5, **126–7**
  chilli con carne 96, **97**
  coda alla vacinnara 114, **115**
  fasolia 62, **63**
  feijoada 150
  Flemish stew 104, **105**
  jardineira 102, **103**
  Kerala beef stew 112–13, **112**
  miso short rib 100, **101**
  oxtail kimchi stew 122, **123**
  potjiekos 106, **107–9**
  rabo de toro 110, **111**
  rendang 120–1, **120**
  sancocho 144–5, **146–7**
  stifado 116, **117**
beetroot 30
Belgium 104
berbere **28**, 29
black bean
  feijoada 150
  Ital stew 60–1
  port wine stew 142
black-eye pea(s)
  harissa black-eye peas 58, **59**
  miso, fennel and squash stew 26
  red bean(s) 52
  waakye rice 207
bo kho 118, **119**
Brazil 150, 178
bread (pre-bought) 48, 104
  bread paste 93
breadfruit 36
broth, mushroom 33
butter, spiced **28**, 29
butter bean 134, **135**
butternut squash 51, 106

cabbage, potjiekos 106
Cajun prawn stew 174, **175**
caldeireda de piexe 176, **177**
callaloo (canned) 36
cannellini bean
  chorizo white bean stew 134, **135**
  fasolia 62
  loubia 44
  puca picante 30
  Tuscan-style bean stew 136, **137**
Caribbean 10, 36, 60–1, 144–5, 180–1, 212
  see also Dominican Republic
carne seca, Brazilian 150
carrot
  aji de gallina 93
  beef bourguignon 98
  bo kho 118
  coda alla vacinnara 114
  daube 56
  frango estufado 76
  Ital stew 60–1
  jardineira 102
  Kerala beef stew 113
  leftover turkey stew 78
  miso, fennel and squash stew 26
  oil down 36
  pollo guisado 91
  potjiekos 106
  rabo de toro 110
  stew lentils 19
cassava
  brown stew lamb 158–9
  encebollado 185
  Ital stew 60–1
  sancocho 144–5
  stew peas 51
  sudado de pollo 68
celery
  aji de gallina 93
  brown stew lamb 159
  Cajun prawn stew 174
  coda alla vacinnara 114

INDEX

celery (cont.)
   red beans Louisiana 140
   sancocho 145
   stew lentils 19
chanfana 164, **165**
chicken
   aji de gallina **92**, 93
   chicken stock 85
   chipotle chicken stew 66–7, **66**
   fesenjan 86, **87**
   frango estufado 76, **77**
   gulai ayum 88
   obe ata 84–5, **84**
   piri piri stew 72, **73**
   pollo guisado (Dominican Republic) 70–1, **70**
   pollo guisado (El Salvador) 90–1, **90**
   sancocho 144–5, **146–7**
   seco de gallina 74, **75**
   sudado de pollo 68, **69**
   tagine mchermel 80–1, **82–3**
chickpea(s)
   chickpea maafe 46, **47**
   chickpea masala **54**, 55
   garbanzos Español 48, **49**
chile Colorado 124–5, **126–7**
chilli con carne 96, **97**
chilli paste 124–5
chipotle chicken stew 66–7, **66**
chorizo
   feijoada 150, **151–3**
   garbanzos Español 48, **49**
   jardineira 102, **103**
   port wine stew 142, **143**
   red beans Louisiana 140, **141**
   white bean stew 134, **135**
chouriço (Portuguese)
   jardineira 102, **103**
   port wine stew 142, **143**
ciambotta 20, **21**
cioppino 190, **191**
cocoa powder 96, 98, 114
coconut (desiccated) 121
coconut cream 113, 121
coconut milk
   chickpea masala 55
   gulai ayum 88
   Ital stew 60–1
   Kerala beef stew 113
   Maldivian tuna stew 192
   miso mushroom stew 24
   moqueca 178

   oil down 36
   rendang 121
   rice and peas 202
   stew lentils 19
   stew peas 51
   stewed saltfish 181
   Thai prawn stew 182
coconut water 118
coda alla vacinnara 114, **115**
Colombia 68
corn-on-the-cob 106, 144–5
courgette 20, 148
cream 78, 188

daube 56, **57**
Dominican Republic 70–1

Ecuador 74, 184–5
egg 138
El Salvador 90–1
encebollado 184–5, **184**
Ethiopia 28–9
evaporated milk 34, 93

fasolia 62, **63**
feijoada 150, **151–3**
fennel, squash and miso stew 26, **27**
fesenjan 86, **87**
feta cheese 34
fish
   caldeireda de piexe 176, **177**
   cioppino 190, **191**
   encebollado **184**, 185
   fiskgryta 188, **189**
   Maldivian tuna stew 192, **193**
   marmitako 172, **173**
   moqueca 178, **179**
   sea bass tagine 196–7, **198–9**
   stewed saltfish 180–1, **180**
flat bean 36
Flemish stew 104, **105**
France 7, 10, 98
frango estufado 76, **77**

garbanzos Español 48, **49**
Georgia 48
ghalieh meygoo 186, **187**
Ghana 32–3, 52
ghormeh sabzi 156–7
goat water 162, **163**
Greece 116
green seasoning (sofrito) 210

brown stew lamb 158–9
habichuelas 132
oil down 36
gulai ayum 88, **89**

habichuelas 132, **133**
haricot bean 60–1
harissa black-eye peas 58, **59**

India 54–5
Indonesia 10, 88, 120–1
Iran 7, 22, 86, 130, 156–7, 186
Ital stew **60**, 61
Italy 20, 114, 136

jackfruit and tarragon stew 38, **39**
Jamaica 50–1, 158–9
Japan 24, 26
jardineira 102, **103**

kale 182
Kerala beef stew 112–13, **112**
kerisik 121
khoresh e khalalt 130, **131**
khoresh gheymeh 22, **23**
kimchi (pre-made)
   oxtail kimchi stew 122, **123**
   sundubu jigaee 138
Korea 122, 138

lamb 129–68
   bamia 154, **155**
   brown stew lamb 158–9, **160–1**
   chanfana 164, **165**
   ghormeh sabzi **156**, 157
   khoresh e khalalt 130, **131**
   lamb tagine 166–7, **166**
   nihari 168, **169**
   tabakh roho 148, **149**
Lebanese 7-spice 208
   bamia 154
   fasolia 62
   tabakh roho 148
Lebanon 62
leek
   arroz de marisco 195
   chorizo white bean stew 134
   encebollado 185
   fiskgryta 188
   miso mushroom stew 24
   miso short rib 100
   rabo de toro 110

lemon (preserved) 58, 80–1, 197
lentejas con calabaza 16, **17**
lentil(s)
   lentejas con calabaza 16, **17**
   misir wat 29
   miso mushroom stew 24
   stew lentils 18–19, **18**
lime
   brown stew lamb 158–9
   chilli con carne 96
   moqueca 178
   puca picante 30
lime (Persian dried black)
   ghormeh sabzi 157
   jackfruit and tarragon stew 38
   khoresh e khalalt 130
   khoresh gheymeh 22
locro de zapallo 34, **35**
loubia 44, **45**

malanga (taro) 144–5
Maldives 10, 192
marinades
   for beef 118, 145
   for chicken 67, 71, 81, 91, 145
   for fish/seafood 197
   for lamb 158–9, 167
   for pork 145
marmitako 172, **173**
Mauritius 56
Mediterranean 10, 194–5
Mexican hominy 34
Mexico 66–7
Middle East 10, 154
misir wat 28–9, **28**
miso
   miso, fennel and squash stew 26, **27**
   miso mushroom stew 24, **25**
   miso short rib 100, **101**
Montserrat 10, 162
moqueca 178, **179**
Morocco 10, 44, 80–1, 166–7, 196–7
Mozambique 72
mushroom
   beef bourguignon 98
   fesenjan 86
   leftover turkey stew 78
   miso mushroom stew 24, **25**
   mushroom broth 33
   potjiekos 106
   Thai prawn stew 182

Nigeria 7, 84–5
nihari 168, **169**
niter kibbeh **28**, 29

obe ata 84–5, **84**
oil down 36, **37**
okra 154
olive(s) (green)
   chorizo white bean stew 134
   habichuelas 132
   sea bass tagine 196–7
   tagine mchermel 80–1
oxtail
   coda alla vacinnara 114, **115**
   oxtail kimchi stew 122, **123**
   potjiekos 106, **107–9**
   rabo de toro 110, **111**

Pakistan 168
pancetta
   chanfana 164, **165**
   habichuelas 132, **133**
Parmesan cheese 93
passata
   arroz de marisco 195
   bamia 154
   caldeireda de piexe 176
   chilli con carne 96
   chipotle chicken stew 67
   chorizo white bean stew 134
   ciambotta 20
   cioppino 190
   coda alla vacinnara 114
   daube 56
   fasolia 62
   frango estufado 76
   habichuelas 132
   jardineira 102
   loubia 44
   marmitako 172
   piri piri stew 72
   qorma a lubia 42
   rabo de toro 110
   red bean(s) 52
   stifado 116
   sudado de pollo 68
   tabakh roho 148
   Tuscan-style bean stew 136
peanut
   puca picante 30
   'relax' 91
peanut butter 46

pea(s)
   chipotle chicken stew 67
   daube 56
   jardineira 102
   rice and peas **160–1**, 202
pecan nut 93
pepper (green)
   arroz de marisco 195
   brown stew lamb 159
   Cajun prawn stew 174
   caldeireda de piexe 176
   chickpea maafe 46
   chilli con carne 96
   encebollado 185
   green seasoning 210
   moqueca 178
   pollo guisado 71
   red beans Louisiana 140
   sancocho 145
   stew lentils 19
   stewed saltfish 181
pepper (habanero), pepper paste 85
pepper (orange)
   ciambotta 20
   pepper paste 85
   stewed saltfish 181
pepper paste 85
pepper (red)
   arroz de marisco 195
   brown stew lamb 159
   caldeireda de piexe 176
   chile Colorado 124–5
   chilli con carne 96
   ciambotta 20
   encebollado 185
   garbanzos Español 48
   green seasoning 210
   marmitako 172
   moqueca 178
   pepper paste 85
   piri piri stew 72
   pollo guisado 71
   sancocho 145
   sea bass tagine 196–7
   seco de gallina 74
   stew lentils 19
   stewed saltfish 181
   sudado de pollo 68
   waakye stew 33
pepper (Romano)
   pepper paste 85
   waakye stew 33

pepper (yellow)
  brown stew lamb 159
  ciambotta 20
  moqueca 178
  sea bass tagine 196–7
  stewed saltfish 181
Persia 48
Persian tahdig **87**, **131**, **156**, **187**, 203
Peru 30, 34, 92–3
pine nut 114
pinto bean 60–1, 132
piri piri stew 72, **73**
plantain (green)
  sancocho 144–5
  tostones 213
pollo guisado (Dominican Republic) 70–1, **70**
pollo guisado (El Salvador) 90–1, **90**
pork 129–64
  chorizo white bean stew 134, **135**
  feijoada 150, **151–3**
  habichuelas 132, **133**
  port wine stew 142, **143**
  red beans Louisiana 140, **141**
  sancocho 144–5, **146–7**
  sundubu jigae 138, **139**
  Tuscan-style bean stew 136, **137**
  see also bacon; chorizo; chouriço (Portuguese); pancetta
port wine stew 142, **143**
Portugal 10, 76, 102, 134, 142, 164, 176
potato
  bo kho 118
  brown stew lamb 158–9
  caldeireda de piexe 176
  chipotle chicken stew 67
  ciambotta 20
  Ital stew 60–1
  jardineira 102
  Kerala beef stew 113
  khoresh gheymeh 22
  leftover turkey stew 78
  marmitako 172
  pollo guisado 91
  sea bass tagine 196–7
  sudado de pollo 68
potjiekos 106, **107**
poultry 65–93

prawn
  Cajun prawn stew 174, **175**
  cioppino 190, **191**
  fiskgryta 188, **189**
  ghalieh meygoo 186, **187**
  moqueca 178, **179**
  sea bass tagine 196–7, **198–9**
  Thai prawn stew 182, **183**
puca picante 30, **31**
Puerto Rico 10, 132
pumpkin
  chickpea masala 55
  habichuelas 132
  lentejas con calabaza 16
  miso, fennel and squash stew 26
  oil down 36
  stew lentils 19
  stew peas 51
  stewed saltfish 181

qorma a lubia 42, **43**
queso fresco 34

rabo de toro 110, **111**
ras el hanout 209
  harissa black-eye peas 58
  marinade for lamb 167
  tagine mchermel 80–1
red beans 52, **53**
red beans Louisiana 140, **141**
red kidney bean
  chilli con carne 96
  daube 56
  ghormeh sabzi 157
  Ital stew 60–1
  qorma a lubia 42
  red beans Louisiana 140, **141**
  rice and peas 202
  stew peas 51
red wine
  beef bourguignon 98
  chanfana 164
  chilli con carne 96
  potjiekos 106
  rabo de toro 110
  stifado 116
'relax' 91
rempah 121
rendang 120–1, **120**
rice
  arroz de marisco **194**, 195
  Persian tahdig **87**, **131**, **156**, **187**, 203

rice and peas **160–1**, 202
vermicelli rice **149**, **155**, 206
waakye rice **32**, 207
runner bean 102, 36

saffron water 211
  arroz de marisco 195
  fesenjan 86
  khoresh e khalat 130
  khoresh gheymeh 22
  oil down 36
  Persian tahdig 203
  tagine mchermel 80–1
salmon, fiskgryta 188, **189**
saltfish, stewed 180–1, **180**
sancocho 144–5, **146–7**
sausage (Italian), Tuscan-style bean stew 136, **137**
sausage (linguiça calabresa), feijoada 150, **151–3**
sausage (Louisiana Andouille), red beans Louisiana 140, **141**
Sazón Goya (with annatto)
  encebollado 185
  habichuelas 132
  'relax' 91
  sudado de pollo 68
sea bass tagine 196–7, **198–9**
seafood 171–97
  arroz de marisco 194–5, **194**
  Cajun prawn stew 174, **175**
  caldeireda de piexe 176, **177**
  cioppino 190, **191**
  encebollado 184–5, **184**
  fiskgryta 188, **189**
  ghalieh meygoo 186, **187**
  Maldivian tuna stew 192, **193**
  marmitako 172, **173**
  moqueca 178, **179**
  sea bass tagine 196–7, **198–9**
  stewed saltfish 180–1, **180**
  Thai prawn stew 182, **183**
seco de gallina 74, **75**
sides 201–7, 212–13
South Africa 106
Spain 9, 10, 16, 48, 110, 134, 172
spices 201, 208–11
  green seasoning (sofrito) 210
  Lebanese 7-spice 208
  ras el hanout 209
  saffron water 211
spinach 48, 157

squash
  chickpea maafe 46
  chickpea masala 55
  Ital stew 60–1
  locro de zapallo 34
  miso, fennel and squash stew 26, 27
  oil down 36
  potjiekos 106
  sancocho 144–5
stew lentils 18–19, **18**
stew peas 50–1, **50**
stifado 116, **117**
stock, chicken 85
sudado de pollo 68, **69**
sundubu jigaee 138, **139**
Sweden 188
sweet potato
  chickpea maafe 46
  chipotle chicken stew 67
  daube 56
  Ital stew 60–1
  potjiekos 106
  stew lentils 19
  stew peas 51
Syria 148

tabakh roho 148, **149**
tagine mchermel 80–1, **82–3**
tahdig, Persian **87**, **131**, **156**, **187**, 203
taro, sancocho 144–5
Thailand 7, 182
tofu 138
tomato
  caldeireda de piexe 176
  chickpea masala 55
  ciambotta 20
  encebollado 185
  garbanzos Español 48
  lamb tagine 167
  marinade 159
  marmitako 172
  misir wat 29
  moqueca 178
  pepper paste 85
  red bean(s) 52
  'relax' 91
  sea bass tagine 196–7
  seco de gallina 74
  stewed saltfish 181
  waakye stew 33
  see also passata

tomato (sun-dried) 134, 172
tostones **69**, 213
Trinidad 18–19
tuna
  encebollado **184**, 185
  Maldivian tuna stew 192, **193**
  marmitako 172, **173**
turkey, leftover turkey stew 78, **79**
Tuscan-style bean stew 136, **137**

UK-inspired recipes 78
USA 96, 124–5, 140, 174, 190

vegetarian stews 15–38
vermicelli rice **149**, **155**, 206
Vietnam 10, 118
waakye rice **32**, 207
waakye stew 32–3, **32**
walnut 86
white wine
  arroz de marisco 195
  caldeireda de piexe 176
  chorizo white bean stew 134
  cioppino 190
  coda alla vacinnara 114
  fiskgryta 188
  frango estufado 76
  jackfruit and tarragon stew 38
  jardineira 102
  leftover turkey stew 78
  Tuscan-style bean stew 136

yellow split pea(s) 22

THANKS

I'd like to begin with a massive thanks to the team at Ebury, without you this book would not exist. Liv and Steph, you are the best! Thank you for all the wonderful advice, vision and support throughout the entire process. As this is my first book, you were unbelievably helpful in guiding me through this new, wonderful and exciting process.

Thank you to Rachel Mills, my superb literary agent who believed in me and helped pitch my idea to Ebury and begin the process of turning this dream into a reality.

Thank you to Harry Bamber, my incredible manager who has guided and supported me throughout my career so far!

My next set of acknowledgements go to everyone who has helped bring the book to life.

Firstly, I'd like to give a massive thanks to the wonderful food stylists, Valerie Berry, Alice Earll and Isobel Macmillan-Scott, who really understood my dream for Stews and it was a real pleasure to be on set with you all. I really appreciate all the precision that was taken with each stew, even if there was a lot of questions to be asked...!

Thank you to the incredible Robert Billington, who captured the true essence of what I wanted my book to be about with a selection of breathtaking images. Thank you for all the care, professionalism and effort that you put into each shot, it truly meant a lot!

Thank you to Abi Wright for designing such an incredible work of art. You captured exactly what I wanted my book to look like and I can't thank you enough for all the hard work and care you have taken on this project.

Thank you to Rachel Vere, for carefully selecting the best set of props that I could have asked for. You really helped bring every image to life.

To Judy Barratt, thank you so much for your patience and all the support you have given me during this journey, I wouldn't have been able to do it without you!

A huge thank you to all my family for being there when I needed them and supporting my dreams. A special thank you to my Nan, who really inspired me to learn how to cook and now 5 years later, I have published my first book. Without you, this book would not have been.

Finally, a massive thank you to all my followers! You all have no idea how grateful I am for each and every one of you that has supported over the past 3 years. Without you all, this would not have been possible. Thank you.

CONVERSION CHARTS

VOLUME	
METRIC	IMPERIAL
25ml	1 fl oz
50ml	2 fl oz
85ml	3 fl oz
150ml	5 fl oz (¼ pint)
300ml	10 fl oz (½ pint)
450ml	15 fl oz (¾ pint)
600ml	1 pint
700ml	1¼ pints
900ml	1½ pints
1 litre	1¾ pints
1.2 litres	2 pints
1.25 litres	2¼ pints
1.5 litres	2½ pints
1.6 litres	2¾ pints
1.75 litres	3 pints
1.8 litres	3¼ pints
2 litres	3½ pints
2.1 litres	3¾ pints
2.25 litres	4 pints
2.75 litres	5 pints
3.4 litres	6 pints
3.9 litres	7 pints
5 litres	8 pints (1 gal)

WEIGHTS	
METRIC	IMPERIAL
15g	½ oz
25g	1 oz
40g	1½ oz
50g	2 oz
75g	3 oz
100g	4 oz
150g	5 oz
175g	6 oz
200g	7 oz
225g	8 oz
250g	9 oz
275g	10 oz
350g	12 oz
375g	13 oz
400g	14 oz
425g	15 oz
450g	1 lb
550g	1¼ lb
675g	1½ lb
900g	2 lb
1.5kg	3 lb
1.75kg	4 lb
2.25kg	5 lb

MEASUREMENTS	
METRIC	IMPERIAL
0.5cm	¼ inch
1cm	½ inch
2.5cm	1 inch
5cm	2 inches
7.5cm	3 inches
10cm	4 inches
15cm	6 inches
18cm	7 inches
20cm	8 inches
23cm	9 inches
25cm	10 inches
30cm	12 inches

OVEN TEMPERATURES			
°C	FAN °C	°F	GAS MARK
140°C	120°C	275°F	Gas Mark 1
150°C	130°C	300°F	Gas Mark 2
160°C	140°C	325°F	Gas Mark 3
180°C	160°C	350°F	Gas Mark 4
190°C	170°C	375°F	Gas Mark 5
200°C	180°C	400°F	Gas Mark 6
220°C	200°C	425°F	Gas Mark 7

EBURY PRESS

UK | USA | Canada | Ireland | Australia
India | New Zealand | South Africa

Ebury Press is part of the Penguin Random House group of companies whose addresses can be found at global.penguinrandomhouse.com

Penguin Random House UK
One Embassy Gardens, 8 Viaduct Gardens, London SW11 7BW

penguin.co.uk

First published by Ebury Press in 2026

1

Copyright © Xavier Bramble 2026
Photography © Rob Billington 2026, except top right photo on page 11, reproduced with permission © Shine TV Limited/Ziji Productions Limited, 2026

The moral right of the author has been asserted.

Penguin Random House values and supports copyright. Copyright fuels creativity, encourages diverse voices, promotes freedom of expression and supports a vibrant culture. Thank you for purchasing an authorised edition of this book and for respecting intellectual property laws by not reproducing, scanning or distributing any part of it by any means without permission. You are supporting authors and enabling Penguin Random House to continue to publish books for everyone. No part of this book may be used or reproduced in any manner for the purpose of training artificial intelligence technologies or systems. In accordance with Article 4(3) of the DSM Directive 2019/790, Penguin Random House expressly reserves this work from the text and data mining exception.

Publishing Director: Stephanie Milner
Senior Editor: Liv Nightingall
Senior Production Manager: Lucy Harrison
Designer: Abi Wright
Production Editor: Nicky Barneby
Photographer: Rob Billington
Food Stylist: Valerie Berry
Prop Stylist: Rachel Vere

Colour origination by Altaimage Ltd
Printed and bound in China by C&C Offset Printing Co., Ltd.

The authorised representative in the EEA is Penguin Random House Ireland, Morrison Chambers, 32 Nassau Street, Dublin D02 YH68.

A CIP catalogue record for this book is available from the British Library

ISBN 9781529953022

Penguin Random House is committed to a sustainable future for our business, our readers and our planet. This book is made from Forest Stewardship Council® certified paper.